CONTENTS

EXPLORING SPACE

THE SOLAR SYSTEM

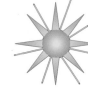

STARS

OUT IN SPACE, BACK IN TIME

COSMIC QUESTIONS

REFERENCE

A Place in the Cosmos

Our ancestors once believed that the Earth must be the centre of the Universe. Every morning they watched the Sun rise in the east and move across the sky. At night the Moon, stars, and planets filled the darkness and all appeared to revolve around the Earth. For almost a thousand years the Church encouraged this view because it placed humans, God's special creation, at the centre. By the 1500s, some astronomers began to argue that the Earth went around the Sun and, in the end, their evidence was overwhelming. Since then we have discovered that the Universe has no real centre. We inhabit one of nine planets orbiting a medium-sized star in a galaxy containing billions of other stars. This galaxy itself is just one among billions of other galaxies. The search for our place in the Universe must be played out on an altogether bigger stage than ever imagined by our ancestors. And that search is the story of this book.

△ Great stone calendars such as Stonehenge, built over 4,000 years ago, helped people keep track of the Sun's daily and yearly movements.

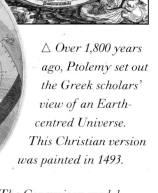

△ Over 1,800 years ago, Ptolemy set out the Greek scholars' view of an Earth-centred Universe. This Christian version was painted in 1493.

△ The Copernican model of the Universe has the Sun at the centre. Copernicus first published his ideas in 1543.

The view from Greece

In 270BC, a Greek philosopher called Anaxagoras suggested that the Earth went round the Sun. His ideas seemed so ridiculous to the people of Athens that he was thrown out of the city! Aristotle's theory, developed by Ptolemy in about AD120, put the Earth at the centre of the Universe with the planets revolving around it in simple circles.

Heavenly revolutions

Nicolaus Copernicus and Galileo Galilei suggested that calculations explaining the motions of planets only made sense if the Earth went around the Sun. Aristotle's model of a Sun-centred Universe was finally overturned in 1610 when Galileo, using his newly invented telescope, discovered that Jupiter had moons orbiting it.

THE KINGFISHER BOOK OF
SPACE

MARTIN REDFERN

KING*f*ISHER

Author Martin Redfern
Consultant Dr Paul Murdin, OBE
Project Editor Clive Wilson
Design Traffika Publishing Limited
Art Editor Susan Aldworth
Picture Researcher Veneta Bullen
Researchers Adam Hibbert, Laura Sheppard
Production Susan Wilmot, Richard Waterhouse
Indexer Hilary Bird

New Penderel House, 283–288 High Holborn, London WC1V 7HZ

First published by Kingfisher Publications Plc 1998
First published in paperback 2000

(hb) 2 4 6 8 10 9 7 5 3 1

2(TR)/0898/TWP/NEW/NYM150

(pb) 2 4 6 8 10 9 7 5 3 1

2(1TR)/0500/TWP/NEW/NYM150

Copyright © Kingfisher Publications Plc 1998

A CIP catalogue record for this book is available from the British Library

ISBN 0 7534 0218 1 (hb)
ISBN 0 7534 0354 4 (pb)

Colour separations by Newsele
Printed in Singapore

True scale of the Universe

Our galaxy (*right*) lies in a tiny corner of the
Universe. The Sun, around which we orbit at an
average distance of 150 million kilometres, is no
more than a dot in one of the Galaxy's spiral
arms. Light takes 100,000 years to reach the
Earth from the other side of the Galaxy and
ten billion years from the furthest galaxies.

▽ *Albert Einstein provided
the framework for our
modern understanding of
the Universe. In 1915, he
proved that space and time
cannot be clearly separated
and space itself is curved.*

△ *Edwin Hubble was the
first person to prove that
there are galaxies other
than our own. In the late
1920s, he showed that the
galaxies are rushing apart
from each other and that
the Universe is expanding.*

Looking Up

In 1609, news reached Italy that a Dutch instrument-maker had used two curved pieces of glass in a tube to magnify a distant object. The first lens focused the object into an image, the second magnified it. The Italian astronomer, Galileo, realized that this 'telescope' could be used to observe the sky, and the heavens became open to serious astronomical study. With this new scientific instrument, Galileo revealed four moons orbiting Jupiter, evidence for the idea that the planets might in turn orbit the Sun. The first telescopes used lenses. Reflecting telescopes, invented in the 1660s, have a concave mirror instead of a lens to focus and catch starlight. The mirror only needs to be curved on one side, so it can be made bigger and detect fainter objects in greater detail.

△ *Galileo's detailed sketches of the Moon were made using the telescope he constructed in 1609.*

▽ *William Herschel's telescope, completed in 1789, was used to study and calculate the distribution of thousands of stars through space.*

▷ *The 100-inch (2.5 m) Hooker Telescope on Mount Wilson, California, remained the biggest and most powerful telescope in the world until 1948.*

◁ The Very Large Array is a series of 27 radio telescopes in the New Mexico desert. Together they have the resolution of an instrument 27 km across, and provide detailed maps of distant galaxies.

◁ The 4.2 metre William Herschel Telescope is built on a high, dry mountain peak on La Palma in the Canary Islands. The lines in the sky are the trails of stars.

Mirror power

A reflecting telescope's power depends on the size of its mirror. The latest generation of telescopes have mirrors over eight metres in diameter. Computers keep the mirrors in alignment. The *Very Large Telescope* in Chile, when it is completed in 2002, will have the power to spot a firefly 10,000 km away.

High and dry

Even on a clear night, the Earth is not a perfect place to put a telescope. Water vapour and turbulence in the atmosphere blur the images and make the stars seem to dance around. In order to avoid this, optical telescopes are usually built on mountains. But even here the window of the Universe is not fully open to astronomers.

Radio waves

Objects in the Universe emit radiation at all wavelengths, from gamma rays to radio waves. Visible light, from red to violet, is just one part of this electromagnetic spectrum. Apart from light, only radio waves can properly penetrate the Earth's atmosphere. Today, individual radio telescopes on different continents are linked by computer to give the equivalent of a single dish thousands of kilometres wide.

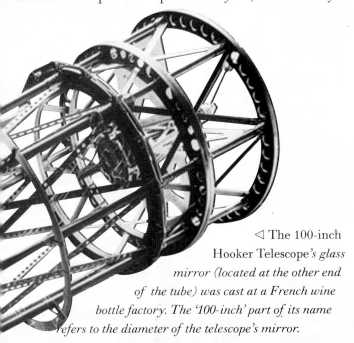

◁ The 100-inch Hooker Telescope's glass mirror (located at the other end of the tube) was cast at a French wine bottle factory. The '100-inch' part of its name refers to the diameter of the telescope's mirror.

▽ Light is only one octave of the great keyboard of the electromagnetic spectrum. Only visible light and part of the radio spectrum penetrate far through the Earth's atmosphere.

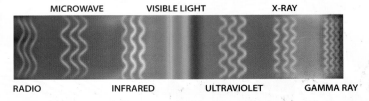

MICROWAVE   VISIBLE LIGHT   X-RAY

RADIO   INFRARED   ULTRAVIOLET   GAMMA RAY

△ High, dry mountain peaks provide the best location for observing the sky. This radio telescope (left) and optical telescope (right) are found at Cerro La Silla in the Andes mountains of Chile.

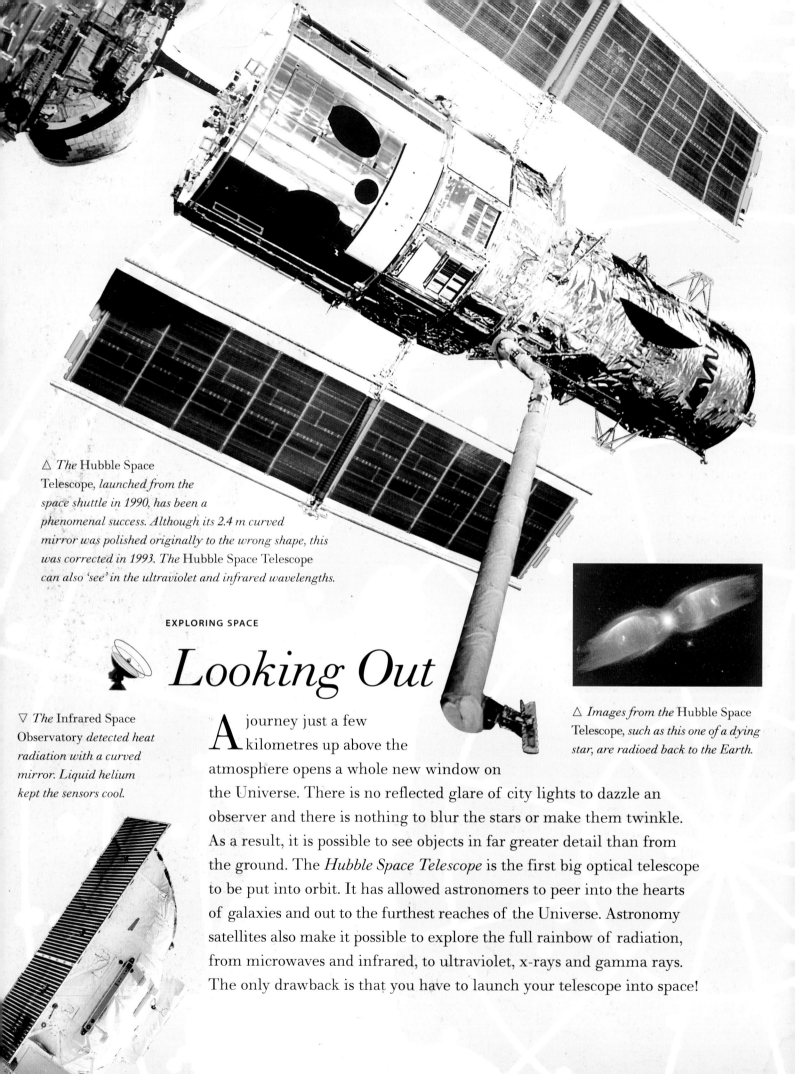

△ *The* Hubble Space Telescope, *launched from the space shuttle in 1990, has been a phenomenal success. Although its 2.4 m curved mirror was polished originally to the wrong shape, this was corrected in 1993. The* Hubble Space Telescope *can also 'see' in the ultraviolet and infrared wavelengths.*

Looking Out

▽ *The* Infrared Space Observatory *detected heat radiation with a curved mirror. Liquid helium kept the sensors cool.*

A journey just a few kilometres up above the atmosphere opens a whole new window on the Universe. There is no reflected glare of city lights to dazzle an observer and there is nothing to blur the stars or make them twinkle. As a result, it is possible to see objects in far greater detail than from the ground. The *Hubble Space Telescope* is the first big optical telescope to be put into orbit. It has allowed astronomers to peer into the hearts of galaxies and out to the furthest reaches of the Universe. Astronomy satellites also make it possible to explore the full rainbow of radiation, from microwaves and infrared, to ultraviolet, x-rays and gamma rays. The only drawback is that you have to launch your telescope into space!

△ *Images from the* Hubble Space Telescope, *such as this one of a dying star, are radioed back to the Earth.*

△ *Launched from the space shuttle* Atlantis, *the* Compton Gamma Ray Observatory *is named after Arthur Holly Compton, an American scientist who pioneered the study of gamma rays.*

Heat detection

Infrared, or heat radiation, comes from warm objects that are not as hot as the stars we see. These include planets and comets, regions where new stars are forming, and distant galaxies ablaze with young stars. Although telescopes located on high mountains can see some infrared radiation, the first comprehensive study came with the *Infrared Astronomy Satellite* (*IRAS*) in 1983. In 1995, Europe's *Infrared Space Observatory* (*ISO*) was launched to look in even greater detail.

Gamma rays

Gamma rays are released by the most energetic processes in the Universe. These include matter falling into a black hole, matter and antimatter annihilating each other and explosions in the cores of galaxies. Launched in 1991, the *Compton Gamma Ray Observatory* is an orbiting laboratory which has detected sudden bursts of gamma rays coming from every direction.

▷ Exosat *was designed to study x-ray sources. Between 1983 and 1986 it made and sent back over 2,000 observations.*

Ultraviolet

Ultraviolet light comes from hot gas and stars. It carries the fingerprints of the atoms that emitted it and the gas clouds through which it has travelled. The *International Ultraviolet Explorer* (*IUE*) was one of the most successful astronomy satellites to date. Launched in 1978 with a planned life of three years, *IUE* focused the light with a 0.5 metre mirror. Instead of taking a picture, it spread the light out into the spectrum of wavelengths, revealing the atomic fingerprints. It was finally switched off in 1997 after nearly nineteen years in service.

△ *The* International Ultraviolet Explorer *was the only ultraviolet observatory in space until the launch of the* Hubble Space Telescope *in 1990.*

Rise of the Rocket

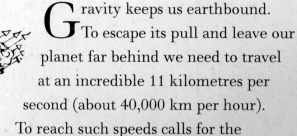

Gravity keeps us earthbound. To escape its pull and leave our planet far behind we need to travel at an incredible 11 kilometres per second (about 40,000 km per hour). To reach such speeds calls for the power of a rocket. The first rockets were more like fireworks and followed the invention of gunpowder by the Chinese in about AD1000. They used rocket-propelled flaming arrows, launched from a basket, against their enemies (*see picture above left*). Warfare continued to be the driving force in the development of rocketry. During World War II, the V2 rockets of Nazi Germany terrorized British cities. Captured V2s were sent to the United States, and their successors, the intercontinental ballistic missiles, helped to launch the space age.

△ *After World War II, captured German V2 rockets, together with their inventor Wernher von Braun, played a key role in the American space programme.*

△ *Robert Goddard designed the first successful liquid-fuel rocket. Its maiden flight in March 1926 lasted 2.5 seconds.*

The pioneers

After the end of World War II, the pace of rocket research accelerated, with Wernher von Braun in the United States and Sergei Korolev in Russia leading the way. A race soon developed between the two superpowers – if a rocket could send a payload into Earth orbit, it could also deliver a bomb to the other side of the world.

◁ *The mighty* Saturn V *rocket lifts off from Cape Canaveral, Florida, on July 16, 1969 to put the first men on the Moon.*

Winners and losers

On October 4, 1957, the Soviet Union demonstrated that they had the edge when they put *Sputnik 1*, a 58-cm aluminium sphere with a radio transmitter, into orbit. Meanwhile, the US Navy *Vanguard* rocket blew up on the launch pad. Wernher von Braun was called in with his army team and, on January 31, 1958, his *Jupiter-C* rocket put *Explorer 1*, America's first satellite, into orbit.

◁ *Rockets often have several stages, each carrying its own oxygen with which to burn the fuel. The first stage of* Saturn V *had five great engines, burning 15 tonnes of kerosene and liquid oxygen every second. It produced a thrust of 3,500 tonnes and lasted for less than three minutes before falling back to the Earth.*

◁ Cosmonaut Yuri Gagarin was the first person to orbit our planet, on April 12, 1961.

△ On November 3, 1957, a Russian dog, Laika, became the first living creature to orbit the Earth. The craft, Sputnik 2, was not designed to return and, after seven days, Laika was injected with poison.

△ A single motor, using liquid hydrogen, fired for two minutes to place the astronauts in Earth orbit, then again to set them on course for the Moon.

▷ Amateur rockets are becoming increasingly sophisticated and successful. With commercial sponsorship, amateurs hope to reach space and launch small satellites.

Spacemen

The first man in space followed shortly after the first satellite. Again, Russia won the race, launching Yuri Gagarin into a single Earth orbit on April 12, 1961. Three weeks later, Alan Shepard became the first American to be blasted into space, though not into orbit, landing 15 minutes later in the Atlantic. Finally, on February 20, 1962, the American John Glenn made three Earth orbits.

△ Two seconds after the first stage broke away, the five rocket motors on the second stage fired, burning liquid hydrogen and liquid oxygen. This stage lasted for six minutes, during which time the escape tower (for use in a launch pad emergency) was jettisoned.

Popular destination

Since the late 1950s, thousands of rockets have been launched and hundreds of people have visited space. But it has never become routine. The dangers are such that each mission involves thousands of people on the ground, checking and re-checking the complex systems of spaceflight.

V2   ATLAS   SOYUZ A2   ARIANE   TITAN IIIE   SPACE SHUTTLE   SATURN V

△ At 110 metres high, Saturn V towers over other rockets. These include the German V2, first used in 1944, and Atlas and Soyuz, which took astronauts into space. The Titan and Ariane rockets launch satellites.

Race to the Moon

As soon as rockets could break away from the Earth's gravity, the next goal became the Moon. It was a whole new world waiting to be explored – and claimed! The Russians again took the lead, landing the first craft on the Moon and photographing the dark, or far, side in 1959. Meanwhile, the United States launched 11 unmanned Moon missions, without one completing its objective. Then, on May 25, 1961, President Kennedy committed the United States to putting a person on the Moon by 1970. The Apollo programme began, and on July 21, 1969, *Apollo 11* landed the first astronauts on the Moon.

△ *From its Earth orbit, the final stage of the* Saturn V *rocket boosts the Command and Service Module (CSM) on its 400,000 km journey (green) to the Moon. The CSM stays in orbit around the Moon while the lunar lander visits the surface. The lander rejoins the CSM for the journey back home (red).*

▷ *Their mission completed, the lunar lander blasts off from the Moon, leaving the bottom half of the lander and a remote camera behind.*

△▷ *One astronaut stays orbiting the Moon in the CSM while the other two enter the lunar lander. The lander makes a vertical descent to the surface, using its single rocket to slow down the craft.*

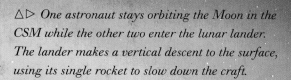

△ *James Irwin salutes the US flag in front of Apollo 15's lander, after returning with a collection of rocks on the lunar rover (right).*

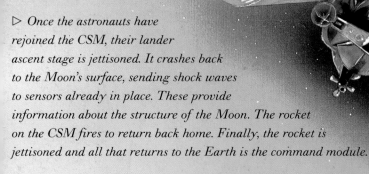

▷ *Once the astronauts have rejoined the CSM, their lander ascent stage is jettisoned. It crashes back to the Moon's surface, sending shock waves to sensors already in place. These provide information about the structure of the Moon. The rocket on the CSM fires to return back home. Finally, the rocket is jettisoned and all that returns to the Earth is the command module.*

Failure rate

From 1959 to 1976 there were 48 Russian and 31 American unmanned Moon missions. Of these, about half failed, but the pressure to get to the Moon was so great that both sides kept on trying. Slowly, reliability improved. Even so, there were a number of casualties. Three US astronauts died when fire broke out in the *Apollo 1* command module and four Russian cosmonauts died during re-entry.

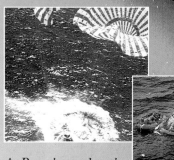

△ *Parachutes slow the command module before splashdown into the ocean. Airbags inflate to keep it upright and the astronauts disembark.*

A change of direction

To land people on the Moon and return them to the Earth required a very powerful and reliable rocket. While the US's *Saturn V* fitted the bill, Russia's *N1* rocket suffered four failures. In 1974, Russia cancelled its programme and concentrated on establishing a permanent presence above the Earth with its space stations.

Houston, we have a problem

On April 13, 1970, *Apollo 13* was 56 hours into its flight when commander Jack Swigert reported, "We have a problem". An oxygen tank had exploded, and the astronauts had to conserve power, air and water for four tense days before they could return to the Earth.

LUNA 2

LUNA 16

SURVEYOR

LUNOKHOD

APOLLO

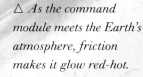

△ *In 1959, Russia's* Luna 2 *became the first space probe to reach the Moon. In 1970, the unmanned* Luna 16 *sent back a capsule with Moon rocks.*

Five US Surveyor craft landed in the 1960s. In 1970, Russia's Lunokhod 1 travelled 10.5 km on the surface. Six Apollo craft landed on the Moon.

△ *As the command module meets the Earth's atmosphere, friction makes it glow red-hot.*

The Space Shuttle

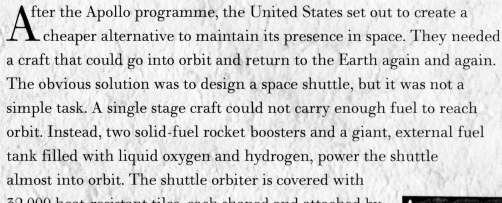

△ *Using a Manned Manoeuvring Unit (MMU) like a sort of jet-propelled armchair, an astronaut can fly freely from the shuttle's cargo bay. The MMU is used to help retrieve faulty satellites, take photographs, or just to admire the view.*

▽ *A space shuttle blasts off from the Kennedy Space Center in Florida. The brilliant jet from the two solid-fuel rocket boosters (one of which is in the foreground) provides five times more thrust than the shuttle's three main engines (on the right).*

After the Apollo programme, the United States set out to create a cheaper alternative to maintain its presence in space. They needed a craft that could go into orbit and return to the Earth again and again. The obvious solution was to design a space shuttle, but it was not a simple task. A single stage craft could not carry enough fuel to reach orbit. Instead, two solid-fuel rocket boosters and a giant, external fuel tank filled with liquid oxygen and hydrogen, power the shuttle almost into orbit. The shuttle orbiter is covered with 32,000 heat-resistant tiles, each shaped and attached by hand, which protect it on re-entry to the atmosphere. *Columbia*, the first operational orbiter, made its maiden flight in April 1981.

Life in orbit

Life aboard a shuttle is more comfortable than that inside the cramped quarters of the Apollo modules. There is a wash room and bunk beds. The food is much better and there is plenty to do, with fantastic views of the Earth just outside the windows. After take-off, the crew (of up to eight people) can wear comfortable clothes. There are racks of experiments in the living quarters. In the cargo bay, satellites can be carried for launch, or retrieved for repair. Astronauts put on space suits and go out through an air lock to work outside the orbiter.

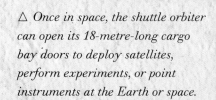

△ *Once in space, the shuttle orbiter can open its 18-metre-long cargo bay doors to deploy satellites, perform experiments, or point instruments at the Earth or space.*

△ *At blast-off, the shuttle's main engines (using fuel from the external tank) and rocket boosters provide thrust equivalent to 140 jumbo jets. Two minutes later the boosters break away. Then the external tank falls away and it is MECO (Main Engine Cut-Off). After the mission is complete, the main engines slow the orbiter and it begins to fall, glowing red from friction on re-entry. It lands like a glider on a runway.*

◁ *Attempts to design a fully reusable spaceplane are now underway. Unlike the shuttle, spaceplanes will be able to take off as well as land on runways like conventional aeroplanes.*

Challenger disaster

No one wants a space mission to fail, but when there are people on board, safety is the most important issue. Launches are often delayed or called off at the last moment because of a slight change in the weather, a minor computer glitch or a faulty sensor. On January 28, 1986, however, one fault proved fatal. A frosty night before the launch of shuttle *Challenger* caused the rubber 'O' rings sealing the sections of its rocket boosters to become brittle. After take-off, a flame from the rockets broke through a seal sending a jet of fire onto the huge external fuel tank. Little more than a minute into the flight, the tank exploded and the seven astronauts were killed.

Satellite triumphs

After the *Challenger* disaster, shuttle missions were suspended for two and a half years. Since then, among the shuttle's biggest triumphs have been the refurbishment and repair of satellites. For example, after its launch in 1990, the *Hubble Space Telescope* was found to be faulty. In 1993, shuttle astronauts retrieved the telescope and repaired it in space.

▽ *One of the two solid-fuel rocket boosters veers away from the exploding wreckage of the* Challenger *shuttle just 73 seconds after lift-off.*

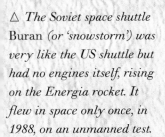

△ *The Soviet space shuttle Buran (or 'snowstorm') was very like the US shuttle but had no engines itself, rising on the Energia rocket. It flew in space only once, in 1988, on an unmanned test.*

Unmanned competition

Although the shuttle is the most versatile manned spacecraft the unmanned satellite launch market is very competitive. The US's leading competitor is the European Ariane rocket, with over 100 successful launches. Russia, China, Japan and India also have rocket programmes.

△ *The* Ariane 5 *rocket sits on its launch pad in French Guiana in June 1996. The first flight was a disaster (a computer fault caused it to veer off course), but the second succeeded. Unlike its rivals,* Ariane 5 *can launch up to four satellites at once.*

▷ *The* International Space Station *as it may look by 2003. Largely US-built and serviced by the space shuttle, it also carries modules from Russia, Europe and Japan.*

△ *Spacelab is a pressurized module that flies in the cargo bay of the space shuttle. On this mission, in 1993, there were around 90 experiments, including ones on the effects of weightlessness on astronauts.*

▽ *Astronauts train underwater* (inset) *to simulate the effects of weightlessness in space and to practise repairing satellites. In space itself, an astronaut uses the shuttle's robot arm like a cherrypicker to control his or her movements above the open cargo bay.*

Living in Space

On May 27, 1973, the space station *Skylab* was launched. Made of modified *Saturn V* and Apollo units, it offered the first long-stay, orbiting laboratory for microgravity research and for studying the Sun and the Earth. It also provided an opportunity to practise space repairs when the crew had to replace damaged shielding. Its last crew set a space endurance record when they spent 84 days living in *Skylab*. In 1977 the Russians launched *Salyut 6*, the first space station to have two airlocks, allowing one crew to arrive before the other departed. This was replaced in 1982 by *Salyut 7* and then, in 1986, by *Mir* in which the endurance record has been broken over and over again.

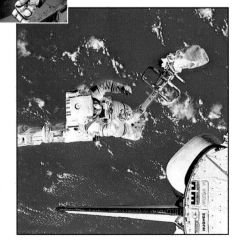

Working in space

In space some of the most difficult tasks are Extra-Vehicular Activities (EVAs). A space suit must be worn as protection from the vacuum, radiation and temperature extremes. Large objects, though weightless, still have mass and, once in motion, can cause havoc. Even turning a screwdriver can cause problems. Unless an astronaut is well-anchored, the screw stays in place while the astronaut rotates!

△ *In July 1995, the US shuttle* Atlantis *docked with* Mir *and both crews posed for cameras. It was the start of a collaboration that provided much-needed cash for Russia's space programme and hardware for the US.*

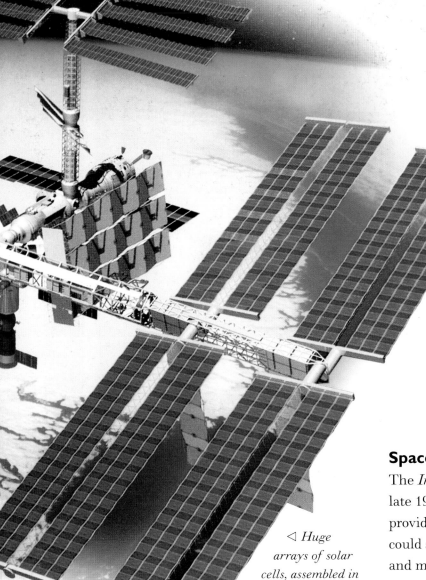

△ *The meals served on board the space shuttle are a great improvement on the dried and concentrated capsules given to Apollo astronauts.*

◁ *This unisex toilet is designed for the* International Space Station. *It comes with foot and thigh restraints. Air flow removes the waste, which is then dried and compressed.*

Space stations of the future

The *International Space Station* is due for launch in the late 1990s. It is a laboratory for microgravity research and provides a testing-ground for future plans. Space stations could serve as assembly points for interplanetary craft and missions to Mars. They could be used as astronomical observatories or even as factories for manufacturing new types of material. A rotating space station with artificial gravity might even one day become a hotel for tourists.

◁ *Huge arrays of solar cells, assembled in space, provide the electrical power for the space station.*

Enduring *Mir*

The core module of the Russian space station *Mir* was launched in 1986 with a planned life of five years. Ten years later, surrounded by add-on modules, it started to show signs of ageing. First, waste water pumps and air conditioning malfunctioned. The oxygen generators failed next, followed by a potentially serious fire which was caused by an oxygen-releasing candle. Then, in June 1997, an unmanned supply craft crashed into one of *Mir*'s modules, cutting forty percent of the power. Only Russian determination and US money kept *Mir* going.

◁ *This close-up of* Mir, *taken from the space shuttle in August 1997, shows damage to a solar array (right) and a thermal radiator (left). The damage was caused by an unmanned Progress supply craft that crashed into* Mir's *Specktr module two months earlier.*

◁ *Since the Russian space station* Mir *was launched in 1986, several new modules have been added to it, increasing its mass from 21 tonnes to over 100 tonnes. Astronauts live and work in the largest module, which is 13 m long. The other modules are used for experiments and storing equipment. Handrails on* Mir's *exterior aid astronauts as they work outside.*

Using Space

Rocket launches are very expensive and not always reliable, yet governments and businesses are queuing up for slots on board launch craft. Space is potentially so useful that it is well worth the risk and expense. Some satellites look at the Earth, following its weather patterns, monitoring the environment, searching for oil and minerals, or even spying on countries. Others are used by astronomers to look out at the stars. The most popular use of space, however, is for communication. In 1945, the writer Arthur C. Clarke predicted that we would communicate via space. This was before the silicon chip was invented, and Clarke imagined vast space stations with teams of engineers to service the unreliable, bulky equipment.

△ *In 1962, Telstar relayed the first live transatlantic TV transmission, which lasted for 20 minutes.*

△ *The Global Positioning System (GPS) uses the signals from at least three satellites to calculate any position on land or at sea.*

▽ *The giant radio dish at Goonhilly Downs, Cornwall, was used to pick up the first transatlantic satellite links.*

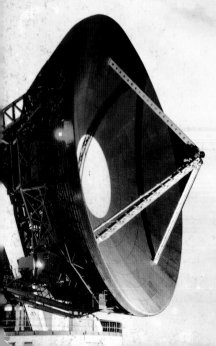

Staying in touch

One of the most popular satellite orbits is called geostationary orbit, 36,000 kilometres above the equator. Here, satellites orbit at the same speed as the Earth rotates, and so always appear to be overhead. But the distance is so great that either a big dish is needed to receive the signal or the signal must be very powerful, and concentrated in a single beam. Now, networks of satellites are launched into low orbit, so there is always one in range of the hand-held receiver of a mobile phone.

△ *The main satellite orbits around Earth are: low Earth orbit (orange), polar orbit (blue), elliptical or Molniya orbit (green), and geostationary orbit (red).*

△ *In 1997, Tony Bullimore spent five days beneath the hull of his capsized yacht. He was saved when satellites located his distress signal.*

Space junk

As more and more rockets and satellites are launched, unwanted junk accumulates in space. Space junk ranges from dropped spanners and chips of paint to spent rocket motors and defunct satellites. The US Air Force is tracking over 8,500 large objects, but even small pieces can be dangerous – a space shuttle window was once chipped, probably by a flake of paint. Operators are encouraged to put old satellites in unused orbits, or force them to burn up in the atmosphere.

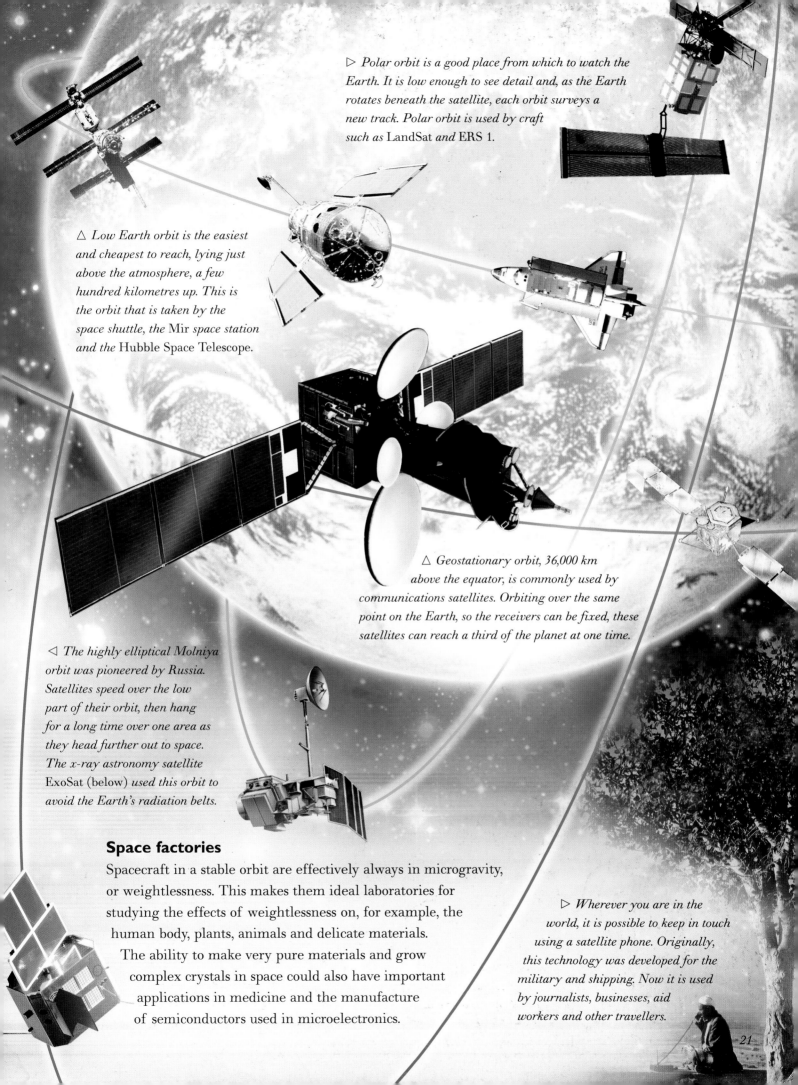

▷ *Polar orbit is a good place from which to watch the Earth. It is low enough to see detail and, as the Earth rotates beneath the satellite, each orbit surveys a new track. Polar orbit is used by craft such as* LandSat *and* ERS 1.

△ *Low Earth orbit is the easiest and cheapest to reach, lying just above the atmosphere, a few hundred kilometres up. This is the orbit that is taken by the space shuttle, the* Mir *space station and the* Hubble Space Telescope.

△ *Geostationary orbit, 36,000 km above the equator, is commonly used by communications satellites. Orbiting over the same point on the Earth, so the receivers can be fixed, these satellites can reach a third of the planet at one time.*

◁ *The highly elliptical Molniya orbit was pioneered by Russia. Satellites speed over the low part of their orbit, then hang for a long time over one area as they head further out to space. The x-ray astronomy satellite* ExoSat (below) *used this orbit to avoid the Earth's radiation belts.*

Space factories

Spacecraft in a stable orbit are effectively always in microgravity, or weightlessness. This makes them ideal laboratories for studying the effects of weightlessness on, for example, the human body, plants, animals and delicate materials. The ability to make very pure materials and grow complex crystals in space could also have important applications in medicine and the manufacture of semiconductors used in microelectronics.

▷ *Wherever you are in the world, it is possible to keep in touch using a satellite phone. Originally, this technology was developed for the military and shipping. Now it is used by journalists, businesses, aid workers and other travellers.*

21

▷ *The Earth is ringed by a cosmic necklace of satellites, watching over it from a range of different orbits.*

Earthwatch

Strangely, we sometimes need to go into space to see our own world more clearly. From the perspective of space it is possible to see the overall pattern without being confused by detail. As long ago as 1948, the astronomer Fred Hoyle commented that "when a photograph of Earth, taken from outside, is returned, an idea as powerful as any in history will be let loose". To a great extent, he was right. Astronauts comment on how fragile the Earth appears from space. Scientists use observations to build up a picture of the complex systems on the Earth and how our environment is changing. Satellite pictures can inspire a sense of wonder, which may generate a new ecological awareness. Space also provides a window for monitoring military activities, along with disaster relief, peace-keeping and humanitarian operations.

△ *From low polar orbit,* Landsat 4 *passes over all points on the Earth. This false-colour image taken over Brazil, shows an area of cleared rainforest with its network of roads.*

△ *Weather satellites hang in geostationary orbit watching weather systems such as this hurricane forming over the Atlantic Ocean. This* Meteosat Second Generation Craft *is designed to help forecasters predict weather in the new millennium.*

△ *The* ERS-2 *satellite measures ozone in the upper atmosphere. Here an ozone hole* (in blue) *is clearly seen above the Antarctic.*

And now for the weather . . .

Satellite images are used in weather forecasts to show us what weather to expect. Weather satellites monitor wind speed, cloud temperature and height, sea temperature, and many other factors. Computers then produce detailed forecasts up to a week ahead. These are vital to farmers, sailors and even ice-cream makers. This data can also help predict climate changes, such as global warming, decades into the future.

△ The space shuttle
sometimes carries remote
sensing instruments for monitoring
the Earth. These two images were
taken by cloud-penetrating radar.
They reveal new flows of ash
and lava on Mount Pinotubo,
an active volcano in the
Philippines.

△ Spy satellites often use
powerful telescopes to watch for
potential threats. Here, a train
carrying Iraqi tanks can be seen
heading towards Kuwait in 1994.

△ ERS satellites use
radar, ultraviolet and infrared to monitor the Earth. Here, two
combined images show ground movements after an earthquake.

Mapping the Earth

In a few 90-minute-long orbits, a satellite can produce a
geological survey of an area of remote and mountainous
country that would take years to map on the ground. By
looking at the ground, not in just the few colours our eyes
can see but using hundreds of different bands of the
spectrum, it is possible to reveal mineral deposits, polluted
areas, and analyze rocks and soil. Satellites can reveal
deforestation or the health of crops. They even detect
rocks deep inside the Earth in the search for new oil fields.

Spy in the sky

One of the first uses of space was for military purposes.
Many rockets were developed to deliver long-range
missiles and more spy satellites may have been launched
than any other type. Many take photographs, while others
monitor secret radio messages or look for signs of missile
launches or bomb tests. In the 1980s, the United States
planned a space-based defence system, called 'Star Wars'.
Before the technology and finance could be resolved, the
Cold War ended and the project was cancelled.

△ The Solar System was born from a cloud of gas and dust. A knot of gas begins to pull other gas around it (1). The cloud heats up and, as it rotates, it contracts and forms into a disc. Energy is lost in jets of matter from the poles (2).

△ A protostar gradually forms at the centre (3) and secondary knots of gas appear in the disc. These will later become the gas giant planets Jupiter, Saturn, Uranus and Neptune.

△ Nuclear processes start up in the star (4) and radiation begins to drive gas and ice out of the inner regions of the disc.

The Solar System

The Solar System is dominated by the Sun, our local star. It is circled by nine planets and their moons, together with countless asteroids and comets. The four planets closest to the Sun – Mercury, Venus, the Earth and Mars – are small, rocky worlds. The next four planets – Jupiter, Saturn, Uranus and Neptune – are gas giants. Finally, there is little Pluto, more like a moon than a major planet. Pluto is the smallest of the planets with a diameter of 2,200 kilometres. Jupiter is the largest, with a diameter of almost 143,000 kilometres. But it is the Sun which dwarfs everything else in the Solar System. If the Sun were the size of a football, then the Earth would be smaller than a pea in comparison. Even if all the matter in all the planets was gathered together into a single ball, you could fit seven hundred of these balls inside the Sun and still have room to spare.

△ The Solar System is nearly formed. The Sun is beginning to shine strongly through its still dusty shroud (5). Planets have formed but the building rubble is still flying around and bombarding the planets.

Dusty birthplace

About five billion years ago, the material that now makes up the Sun and planets was a great cloud of gas and dust called the solar nebula. This material was composed of a mixture of light elements, mostly hydrogen and helium that had been left over from the formation of our Milky Way galaxy, and heavier elements spewed out by an earlier generation of short-lived stars. A shock wave may have passed through the nebula as it crossed a spiral arm of the Galaxy or as a nearby star exploded. As a result, the nebula began to condense into a nursery of stars.

◁ The inclined orbit of Pluto, together with those of Neptune, Uranus, Saturn and Jupiter are clearly visible. Much further in are the inner planets – Mars, the Earth, Venus and Mercury.

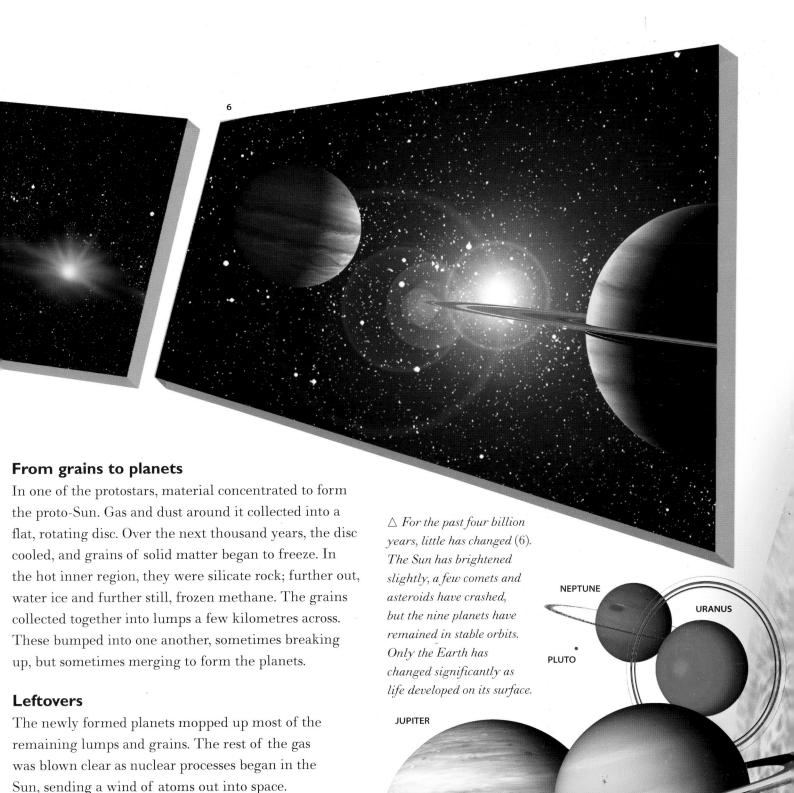

From grains to planets

In one of the protostars, material concentrated to form the proto-Sun. Gas and dust around it collected into a flat, rotating disc. Over the next thousand years, the disc cooled, and grains of solid matter began to freeze. In the hot inner region, they were silicate rock; further out, water ice and further still, frozen methane. The grains collected together into lumps a few kilometres across. These bumped into one another, sometimes breaking up, but sometimes merging to form the planets.

Leftovers

The newly formed planets mopped up most of the remaining lumps and grains. The rest of the gas was blown clear as nuclear processes began in the Sun, sending a wind of atoms out into space. In the outermost reaches of the solar nebula, the icy proto-planetary material was spread so thinly that it did not form planets but remains to this day as a vast cloud of potential comets.

▷ *The Sun and planets are shown here to scale. The Sun dwarfs everything else in the Solar System, including the gas giants Jupiter and Saturn.*

△ *For the past four billion years, little has changed (6). The Sun has brightened slightly, a few comets and asteroids have crashed, but the nine planets have remained in stable orbits. Only the Earth has changed significantly as life developed on its surface.*

NEPTUNE

URANUS

PLUTO

JUPITER

SATURN

MERCURY

VENUS

EARTH

MARS

Mercury

Mercury, named after the Roman winged messenger of the gods, is an elusive planet. Small, fast-moving and lying closer to the Sun than any other planet, it is only visible from the Earth just after sunset or just before dawn. Mercury is the second smallest planet and only slightly larger than our Moon. It takes just 88 Earth days to orbit the Sun. Its distance from the Sun varies from 46 million kilometres at its closest to 70 million kilometres at its most distant. The Sun's strong gravitational tug on Mercury has dramatically slowed the planet's rotation on its axis. As a result, a day on Mercury lasts the equivalent of 176 Earth days – twice as long as its quicksilver 88-day year.

△ Almost everything we know about Mercury comes from one space probe, Mariner 10, *which flew past the planet in 1973, 1974 and again in 1975. Here,* Mariner 10 *is shown above a false-colour image of Mercury's cratered surface.*

▽ Mercury's dry and airless surface creates a very bleak landscape. Pockmarked with impact craters, during the day it is baked by radiation and heat from the nearby Sun.

Unchanged features

The surface of Mercury is very similar to the Moon's. It is heavily cratered, with evidence of ancient lava flows. With no atmosphere or water to erode them, the craters look almost as fresh as the day they were formed. Yet that must have been more than 4 billion years ago, when debris left over from the formation of the planets was still flying about in the Solar System. This rubble crashed into the surface, throwing up circular craters with characteristic central peaks.

△ There is evidence from radar images that there may be ice in the craters near Mercury's poles. In deep craters, icy deposits – possibly left-over material from comet impacts – would remain hidden from the Sun's intense heat.

World of extremes

Mercury has no atmosphere (except for a trace of helium given off by the rocks), so there is no wind or rain. There is also no protection against the Sun's searing heat by day, and no blanket to keep the surface warm at night. With days and nights each lasting about three of the Earth's months, and with the planet swinging closer and farther from the Sun, temperatures can range from 420°C to −180°C. These extremes are hot enough to melt some metals or cold enough to freeze air.

◁ △ More than 4 billion years ago, a huge object must have struck Mercury (above), melting part of the surface and causing ridges and hills to form on the opposite side of the planet. The ridges around the impact crater, called the Caloris Basin (left), were photographed by Mariner 10.

△ *Although only about a third the size of the Earth, Mercury is almost as dense. This suggests that a core of iron-nickel takes up about 70 percent of the interior, with a mantle of silicate rock surrounding it. The outer part of the metal core may still be molten.*

Wizened world

A surprise discovery by *Mariner 10* was a magnetic field on Mercury. The planet had been thought to rotate too slowly for it to generate a magnetic field. The answer may lie in the planet's large core. If the outer part of the core is still molten, currents in it could produce a weak magnetic effect. A big iron core could also explain Mercury's wrinkles. As it cooled and solidified, the iron shrank, making the planet contract and producing a wrinkled appearance on the surface.

Venus

Venus, the brightest planet visible from the Earth, is named after the goddess of beauty. The planet has also been called the Earth's twin. It is almost exactly the same size, is only slightly less dense and is made up of volcanic rocks, but there the similarity ends. The thick atmosphere on Venus means that it is always cloudy, and the pressure on the surface is ninety times greater than on the Earth. The dense atmosphere consists mostly of carbon dioxide – this traps the planet's heat causing a runaway greenhouse effect that makes the worst predictions of global warming on the Earth seem chilly by comparison. The surface temperature is 480°C and if oceans ever existed on Venus they have long since boiled away. If you could withstand the searing heat and bone-crushing pressure on this hostile planet, you would see an orange sky. If it ever rained, you would be drenched in a lethal downpour of sulphuric acid.

△ *Bands of thick, swirling clouds circle Venus at speeds of up to 360 km/h. This ultraviolet picture was taken by* Mariner 10 *in 1974.*

△ *Four Russian Venera probes have landed on Venus and sent back images. In 1982, close-ups taken by* Venera 13 *revealed flat, eroded terrain southeast of a volcanic region called Phoebe Regio. The edge of the Venus lander and its lens cap can also be seen in the picture.*

△ *The* Magellan *radar mapper revealed that the surface of Venus has rough, mountainous terrain* (bright areas) *and smoother plains* (darker areas).

Global warming

The dramatic contrast with the Earth could simply be because Venus is closer to the Sun. As the young Sun warmed, more carbon dioxide was released from Venus' volcanoes and the surface temperature climbed. The seas began to evaporate, the water vapour adding to the greenhouse effect. Without oceans and plants, carbon dioxide could not be removed as the heat output of the Sun continued to grow. On the Earth, billions of tonnes of carbon are locked up in limestone and chalk. On Venus it is all still in the atmosphere.

Revealing geology

The radar mapper on the *Magellan* space probe indicated clear evidence of volcanic activity, including domes of thick or viscous lava and vast floods of liquid basalt. However, it did not detect any drifting plates, which on the Earth create great chains of volcanoes. There must be other forces at work on Venus, still to be identified.

▽ *The landscape is a computer-generated view of Maat Mons, one of the largest volcanoes on Venus. This image was created by radar data sent back by the Magellan probe. The fresh lava flows surrounding this 8-km-high volcano suggest relatively recent activity.*

▷ *The* Magellan *probe, seen here as it was released from the space shuttle in 1989, was made up of spare parts from other missions.*

△ *The existence of uneroded craters on Venus indicate that some parts of the surface are much older than areas covered by volcanic lava. The largest of these craters (top left) has a diameter of 50 km.*

△ *This corona, or circular feature, is about 200 km in diameter. It was probably caused by a rising dome of lava from deep below the surface.*

△ *Like the Earth, Venus has a rocky mantle and a crust. Inside is an iron core that may be partly molten. Because the planet rotates very slowly (unlike the Earth), there is no noticeable magnetic field.*

◁ *The atmosphere of Venus is 96% carbon dioxide. Nitrogen, water vapour and traces of other gases such as sulphur dioxide are also present.*

Lengthy days

Venus is best seen from the Earth with the naked eye just after sunset or before dawn. Like the Moon, Venus has phases as the Sun illuminates a crescent, half or full disc. Venus has a slow rotation from east to west. In fact, its rotation rate of 243 Earth days makes a day on Venus longer than the planet's year – the time it takes to revolve once around the Sun.

29

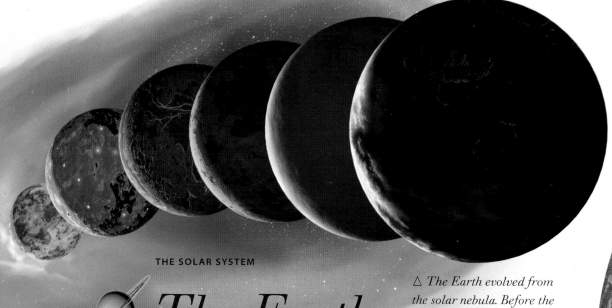

△ The Earth evolved from the solar nebula. Before the atmosphere formed, impacts made it a hot, volcanic planet.

The Earth

△ Charged particles from the Sun rain down near the Earth's poles, creating the spectacular Northern and Southern Lights, or aurora.

The Earth is the planet we call home. Almost every astronaut who has seen it from space has been deeply moved by how beautiful and unique it looks, veiled by a gossamer-thin atmosphere of white cloud and blue haze. Even alien observers would recognize that the Earth is special. The presence of liquid water oceans, ice caps and clouds of water vapour suggests a narrow range of temperatures that are just right for life. An abundance of life using photosynthesis to trap carbon dioxide and release oxygen ensures that levels of oxygen and ozone in the atmosphere remain stable. Without this process the greenhouse effect would spiral out of control. The Earth is a planet that teems with living things and is largely controlled by them.

The young Earth

Around 4.6 billion years ago, the early Earth may have had a thick atmosphere, but the solar wind and intense heat of meteorite impacts soon stripped this away. The interior separated out into a metallic core, a thick mantle of silicate rocks and a crust of lighter silicates. Once the surface had cooled down, a rain of comets probably provided most of the water now in our oceans.

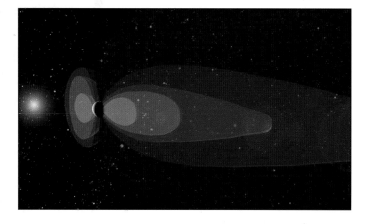

△ The Earth ploughs through the solar wind like a ship, its magnetic field extending into surrounding space. This magnetic envelope, or magnetosphere, is pushed up into a wave in front and trails a long wake.

▷ On the Earth all three forms of water (ice, liquid and vapour) are found. Together, they help provide a climate that is just right for life.

△ *Beneath a thin silicate crust, the Earth has a solid rocky mantle, an outer core of molten iron and a solid iron inner core. When the thin ocean crust dives back down into the mantle, it triggers volcanic eruptions* (above right).

▷ *The Earth's atmosphere extends out more than 100 km. It is made up of 77% nitrogen, 21% oxygen and a small amount of other gases.*

Life appears

The first primitive life forms may have developed in shallow pools, or perhaps around hydrothermal vents. Life may even have been seeded from space on fragments of meteorite or comet. Soon, bacteria and viruses were joined by algae which began to transform the atmosphere by using up carbon dioxide and releasing oxygen. Finally, more than four billion years later, intelligent life developed.

Below the crust

The inside of the Earth is still hot. The molten outer core of iron generates electrical currents which produce the planet's magnetic field. The bulk of the planet, the mantle, is silicate rock. It is solid but hot and is able to distort and flow rather like ice in a glacier. The continents float and drift on the mantle. Where the mantle is hottest, it rises and forms new ocean crust. The ocean floor cools and eventually sinks back into the mantle. All this means that the entire surface of the Earth is made up of a series of plates, edged with volcanoes and earthquake zones.

△ *The Earth is a medium-sized planet with a thick atmosphere. Great stretches of water cover three-quarters of the surface.*

△ *Europe's four* Cluster *probes fly in formation through the Earth's magnetosphere, plotting the planet's interactions with the solar wind.*

The Moon

The Moon is the most spectacular object in the night sky and the only world beyond the Earth so far on which people have walked. It is our closest neighbour, orbiting our planet with the same face always pointing towards us. The far side is often called the dark side because it cannot be seen from the Earth. In its monthly orbit, the Moon seems to change shape as different areas of its surface are lit by the Sun. There are five distinct phases called new, crescent, quarter, gibbous and full. When the side we see is dark (a new Moon) the far side is in full sunshine. The Moon is close enough to the Earth for its gravity to pull the water in the oceans towards it, causing the tides.

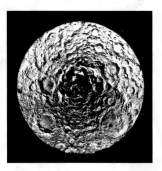

△ *This mosaic of 1,500 images shows the south pole of the Moon. The dark crater in the centre is permanently in shade and contains an icy layer.*

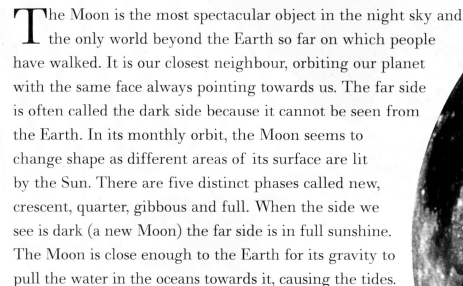

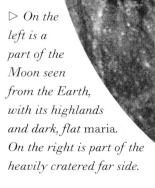

How the Moon formed

There are several theories to explain how the Moon formed. It may have formed together with the Earth from the solar nebula, or perhaps it spun off from a bulge at the Earth's equator. The most popular theory, derived from analysis of Moon rock and computer simulations, is that the early Earth was hit by a protoplanet the size of Mars. Some of the resulting debris merged to form the Moon.

▷ *On the left is a part of the Moon seen from the Earth, with its highlands and dark, flat maria. On the right is part of the heavily cratered far side.*

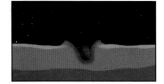

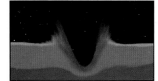

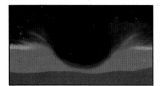

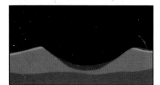

△ *Craters were formed when asteroids plunged into the lunar surface. They can be anything from metres to hundreds of kilometres across.*

△ *This view of the Moon's craters, lit by sunlight at a low angle, was taken from* Apollo 13 *in 1970.*

▷ *The five different phases of the Moon depend on the direction from which it is illuminated by the Sun. During each monthly cycle it goes through nine different stages.*

The Moon's surface

The lunar highlands are more than 4.2 billion years old and heavily cratered. Collisions with asteroids were violent enough to melt parts of the Moon's surface, flooding the impact basins with lava and creating great dark regions called *maria*, or seas. Curiously, there are virtually no such features on the far side of the Moon. About 3.8 billion years ago, the asteroid bombardment virtually ceased, apart from the creation of a few craters such as Copernicus. Without wind and water to erode the surface, the Moon has remained the same ever since.

NEW MOON   WAXING CRESCENT   FIRST QUARTER   WAXING GIBBOUS

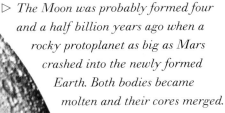

▷ *The Moon was probably formed four and a half billion years ago when a rocky protoplanet as big as Mars crashed into the newly formed Earth. Both bodies became molten and their cores merged.*

▷ *The vaporised rock and fragments from the collision formed a ring around the Earth. Some of the material combined to make an object massive enough to sweep up the debris with its gravity. Finally, only two bodies remained in this area of the Solar System – the Earth and its new Moon.*

Tomorrow's Moon

Twelve men have walked on the Moon, leaving landers, rovers, flags and footprints behind. And it is still the goal of many scientists and commercial enterprises. With only one-sixth of the Earth's gravity, the Moon would be a very good place to mine bulk materials for launch into space. With permanently dark skies, no atmosphere and no radio noise, it would also be an excellent site for setting up telescopes. Water, discovered frozen in the rocks of the poles, could be used to supply moonbases. The main obstacle, at present, is the cost.

◁ *In the future, the low gravity would make moonbases good staging-posts for interplanetary journeys. And the Moon's airless surface and dark skies would make an excellent laboratory for astronomers and scientists.*

△ *There is a thin crust of lighter-coloured granite-like rock on the highlands of the Moon, above a thick, dark, denser rocky mantle.*

FULL MOON **WANING GIBBOUS** **LAST QUARTER** **WANING CRESCENT** **OLD MOON**

Mars

Mars is smaller, darker and slightly more distant than Venus. It is also the most Earth-like of the planets and has always attracted humans. Mars' reddish colour (with its associations of blood) led to it being named after the Roman god of war and Martians have featured in countless science fiction stories. Speculation about life on Mars was reinforced by changing hues on the surface and reported sightings of canals. When the first Mariner probes flew past in the 1960s, however, all they saw was a barren, cratered surface, rather like the Moon, beneath an atmosphere one hundredth the density of the Earth's.

In 1971, *Mariner 9* (the first craft to orbit a planet other than the Earth) explored Mars' fascinating geology. As the dust from a violent storm settled, a giant volcano was revealed, followed by valleys and canyons.

△ *This picture of Mars was taken by the* Hubble Space Telescope *in 1990. It reveals wispy storm clouds around the north pole and thin dust clouds in the south.*

△ *The* Mars Global Surveyor *reached Mars' orbit in September 1997 and began mapping the planet with high resolution cameras, lasers and radar.*

◁ *Mars has two tiny moons, Phobos* (top) *and Deimos* (bottom). *Both are probably captured asteroids. Phobos is heavily cratered. Deimos is smoother and darker.*

Heat and dust

Like Earth, Mars has a 24-hour day, although its year is nearly twice as long. The thin atmosphere is made almost entirely of carbon dioxide. Swirls of cloud are often visible and, in winter, polar caps of water ice and frozen carbon dioxide form. Temperatures range from a comfortable 25°C in summer to a bitter −120°C on winter nights. Although it no longer rains, there is clear evidence that water once flowed on Mars, scouring out deep channels. Today, strong winds whip up dust storms, which sometimes envelop the whole planet.

△ *Mars has a weak magnetic field, suggesting that its core must be solid. The thick rocky mantle may circulate slowly beneath a thin, hard crust.*

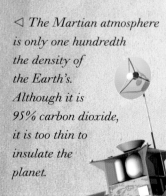

◁ *The Martian atmosphere is only one hundredth the density of the Earth's. Although it is 95% carbon dioxide, it is too thin to insulate the planet.*

▷ *Unlike Mars' south pole, which is mostly frozen carbon dioxide, its north pole is mostly water ice. Every summer it shrinks leaving a spiral pattern, probably due to wind erosion.*

◁ *Two Viking Landers touched down on Mars in 1976. The sampling arm (front left) scooped up soil for analysis. The two cylinders with vertical slits are stereo cameras.*

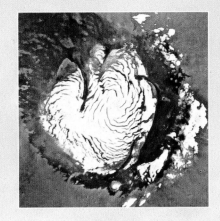

▷ *Evidence shows that water once flowed down this valley in the Valles Marineris.*

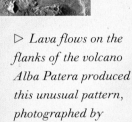

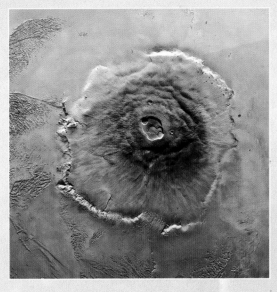

▷ *Lava flows on the flanks of the volcano Alba Patera produced this unusual pattern, photographed by Viking 2's orbiter.*

△ *The Ophir Chasm, in the Valles Marineris, was formed by geological faulting. It has cliffs which are over 4,000 m high. These have seen major landslides, including an avalanche that travelled 65 km.*

△ *The biggest volcano on Mars, and in the Solar System, is Olympus Mons. Like the Earth's biggest volcanoes, it is shield-shaped, and once erupted runny, black, basalt lava. It towers 26,400 m high.*

Vikings invade Mars

By the 1970s it was clear that Mars was neither covered in lush vegetation nor populated by Martians. But there might be microscopic life (bacteria or algae) in the soil. In 1976, two Viking space probes set out to investigate. Each comprised an orbiter and a lander. Both landers contained miniature laboratories to test Martian soil samples for signs of life. They fed nutrients into the soil and, when a gas was given off, it suggested that living organisms were using up the nutrients. But the process slowed and stopped. Scientists concluded that all they had detected were lifeless chemical reactions.

The Martian landscape

Some parts of Mars are heavily cratered and very old. Other parts have been smoothed over by newer lava flows from volcanoes. Cracks and canyons indicate past earthquakes. The Valles Marineris canyon (*below*) is four times deeper and six times wider than the Grand Canyon in the US. There are large areas of wind-blown sand dunes. Dust storms change the surface dramatically, covering or exposing rock underneath. Signs of water erosion suggest past flooding along channels and plains. This water may have escaped to space or lie frozen underground.

△ *A panorama taken by* Viking 2 *in the Utopia Planitia region. The sloping ground is strewn with angular lumps of dark, volcanic rock and frosted with a thin layer of water ice.*

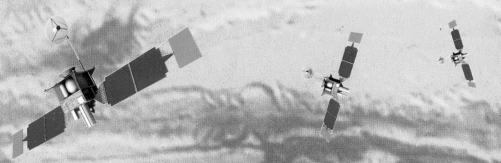

Mission to Mars

The year 1997 marked the return to the red planet. For almost twenty years, every Mars mission had ended in failure. The two Russian *Phobos* craft failed, the US *Mars Observer* exploded as it prepared to enter the planet's orbit and the mighty Russian *Mars '96* craft did not escape from the Earth. But finally, on American Independence Day 1997, *Mars Pathfinder* parachuted down to Mars, its novel landing technology proving a success. Its little six-wheeled rover, *Sojourner*, spent nearly three months analyzing Martian rocks before the battery went flat. More missions have been planned, including a mission to return rock samples to the Earth and ultimately one to land the first humans on Mars.

△ *As* Mars Pathfinder *neared the surface, the tether to its parachute was cut and balloons inflated. The craft bounced to a standstill and opened up to reveal instruments, solar cells and a little rover* (inset below).

Where did all the water go?

Great floods of water once washed down in channels from the Martian highlands and fanned out on the plains below. Now it has all escaped to space, or lies frozen underground or in the icecaps. For water to flow, Mars must once have been warmer and have had a denser atmosphere. About three billion years ago all that changed. The once-molten iron core may have solidified, or the planet been struck by an asteroid. Whatever the cause, it resulted in the cold, barren world we see today.

Meteorite from Mars

In 1984, a grapefruit-sized lump of rock was found in Antarctica. After years of careful research, scientists were able to tell its story. It had formed on Mars 4.5 billion years ago, when the planet was still young. Then, 16 million years ago, an impact threw it out into space, and 13,000 years ago it landed on the Earth. The meteorite contains chemicals and microscopic structures that some NASA scientists suggest are evidence of life — fossils from another world.

▽ Mars Pathfinder *landed in a wide flood plain. The camera revealed a panorama of low hills, and a surface littered with rocks of all sizes and textures for the rover* Sojourner *to analyze.*

▷ *A Martian hand reaches out from a spaceship in the* film The War of the Worlds.

◁ Sojourner *used an x-ray spectrometer to measure the composition of rocks. Here, it is examining the rock given the name 'Barnacle Bill'.*

◁ *The six-wheeled* Sojourner, *the size of a microwave oven, moved from rock to rock, navigating with its own camera and laser, as well as instructions from the Earth.*

△ *AH84001* (left) *is a Martian meteorite that was found in Antarctica. It contains possible fossil evidence of life. Under a powerful electron microscope, a segment of rock reveals structures that could be tiny fossil bacteria* (above).

Alien invaders

Evidence on the Earth suggests that life can endure extremes of temperature and even survive in cracks within rocks. Although Mars appears to be a barren planet, life may once have thrived there in similarly hostile conditions. Fossil hunters of the future will want to explore any ancient hydrothermal springs they may find on Mars. Returned samples are likely to be put into quarantine – just in case microbes are still alive and choose to invade the Earth!

Home from home

Sending people to Mars – and returning them to the Earth – might be more feasible if the fuel for the return journey were to be made on Mars. A robot craft could make propellant from the Martian atmosphere before astronauts arrived. More fanciful is the idea of using orbiting mirrors to warm the South Pole of Mars. This would release more carbon dioxide to warm the planet. Bacteria might release oxygen and ultimately make the atmosphere breathable by human colonists.

▽ *In the distant future, Mars may be made more Earth-like. A thicker atmosphere and warmer climate would allow liquid water to remain on the surface – just as it did some four billion years ago.*

The asteroid belt, between Mars and Jupiter, contains rocks of all sizes. Although they frequently collide and break up, the belt is made up mostly of empty space. All together the asteroids would form an object smaller than the Moon.

Asteroids & Meteorites

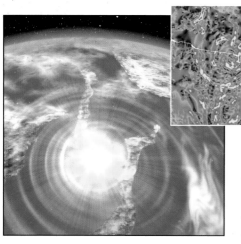

△ *On June 30, 1908, a huge fireball exploded near Tunguska, Siberia flattening more than 3,000 km² of forest. It was probably caused by an asteroid exploding in the atmosphere.*

Between the orbits of Mars and Jupiter is a gigantic belt made up of more than 4,000 lumps of rock. They range in size from a few metres across to the biggest, called Ceres, which is about 1,000 km across. These chunks of rock are called asteroids. Scientists believe they were formed from material similar to that of the rocky planets, such as the Earth and Mars. Stirred up by the immense gravitational influence of Jupiter, this material was unable to stick together to form a single planet. However, mini-planets with iron cores may have formed, only to be smashed up by impacts with smaller debris. Collisions between asteroids are thought to be quite frequent. Some of the asteroids are composed mostly of iron, like the core of the Earth.

◁ *When a large asteroid hit Central America 65 million years ago, it caused a great fireball and climate change that may have ended the age of the dinosaurs. A satellite map (inset) of the Yucatan peninsular, Mexico, shows the rim of the 180-km-wide crater.*

A big impact

Not all asteroids remain in orbit between Jupiter and Mars. Some have elliptical orbits that bring them close to the Earth. Craters on the Moon were caused by asteroid impacts. Asteroids must have bombarded the Earth too, but most of that evidence has eroded. Geologists have identified the traces of enormous ancient craters.
One in the Gulf of Mexico was caused by an asteroid 30 km across that fell 65 million years ago. It threw up thousands of tonnes of water and rock, shutting out the Sun and contributing to the extinction of the dinosaurs.

Could it happen again?

Occasionally, asteroid-sized rocks still hit the Earth. Small asteroid strikes may occur once every 100 years, probably over uninhabited land or sea. A two-km-sized object may hit only once in a million years, but it could change the climate and, indirectly, kill millions of people. Telescopes now look out for rocks that pose a threat, in the hope that missiles or lasers can be used to deflect them.

▷ *Wolf Creek crater* (above) *in Western Australia was formed about 10,000 years ago and still looks fresh. Deep Bay* (below) *in Reindeer Lake, Canada, is 150 million years old. It is so eroded that it was not thought to be an impact crater until 1957.*

Meteorites

Hundreds of tonnes of rock hurtle towards the Earth each year, but most burn up in the atmosphere to form shooting stars. Lumps that reach the surface are called meteorites. A few are chips off comets, the Moon or even Mars, but most are asteroid debris. Collectors scour Australia and Antarctica to recover them. Even the bigger ones, which vaporize on impact, leave traces. Meteorites can enrich sediments many kilometres away.

△ *The commonest meteorites are stony ones made of silicate rocks (1). Glassy tektites (2) form on impact from vaporized rock. Meteorites made of iron (3 and 4) are rarer.*

△ *Metallic asteroids may be very valuable due to the iron, copper, cobalt and nickel they contain. This imaginary scene shows one captured for mining in orbit around the Earth.*

◁ *Under the microscope, a thin slice of meteorite reveals crystals formed at high temperatures, surrounded by dark, carbon-rich material created at lower temperatures.*

Jupiter

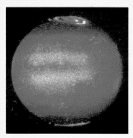

△ *This ultraviolet image shows the glow at Jupiter's poles, as charged particles from the Sun stream along its magnetic field lines.*

Jupiter is the giant among the planets. If all the others were combined, they would still not add up to half of Jupiter's mass. It is a great gas bag made up of 90 percent hydrogen, with a lower density than the Earth. Down in its thick atmosphere, the pressure rises to a point where hydrogen behaves as a liquid rather than a gas. Deeper still, it is like a liquid metal, with huge circulating electrical currents. Here, a powerful magnetic field is generated, strong enough to emit radio waves that can be received on the Earth. Jupiter is still contracting from its formation, a process that generates heat and makes it glow in the infrared. If Jupiter were much bigger, the heating would start nuclear fusion in its core and the planet would become a star.

Turbulent planet

Jupiter's incredibly fast 9 hour 55 minute rotation (or day) makes it bulge 9,000 kilometres wider at its equator than its poles. It whips up violent winds and stretches the clouds out into bands parallel to the equator. Essentially, there are about 14 alternating bands of dark, low pressure regions that circulate with the planet's rotation, and light, high-pressure regions blowing the other way. Swirling storm systems form where they meet, especially in the turbulent polar regions. High white clouds of ammonia ice are tinted yellow and orange lower down by sulphur compounds.

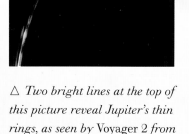

△ *Two bright lines at the top of this picture reveal Jupiter's thin rings, as seen by* Voyager 2 *from a distance of 1,450,000 km.*

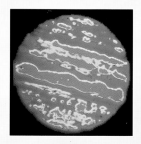

△ *The red bands in this infrared image are gases from the deeper atmosphere, heated by the planet's continued contraction.*

◁ Voyager 2 *went on a grand tour of the giant planets, passing Jupiter in 1979, Saturn in 1981, Uranus in 1986 and Neptune in 1989.*

Cosmic fireworks

In 1993, comet hunters David Levy and Gene and Carolyn Shoemaker spotted a strange comet. It had come so close to Jupiter that gravitational forces had torn it apart into what looked like a string of pearls. Calculations showed that the fragments would crash into the planet (*left*) in July 1994. No one knew what to expect. The impacts would be just out of sight over Jupiter's horizon, so perhaps nothing would be seen. In fact, the fireballs were clearly visible and, as the impact sites rotated into view, they were revealed as great brown marks larger than the Earth.

△ *The Red Spot, a 40,000 km storm system, has been raging for over 300 years. It has a dramatic effect on surrounding weather systems* (inset). *Nearby white ovals are huge temporary storms.*

Visitors to Jupiter

Five spacecraft have visited Jupiter. *Pioneer 10* and *11* and *Voyager 1* and *2* sped past, giving valuable but tantalizingly brief glimpses (they discovered a thin ring of particles as fine as smoke.) But, in December 1995, *Galileo* went into orbit around the giant planet. Although the spacecraft's main antenna failed to open properly, *Galileo* has still returned spectacular pictures and data. On arrival, it released a probe that descended into Jupiter's atmosphere before being destroyed by the heat. The probe found less water than was expected, but it may just have missed the moist clouds.

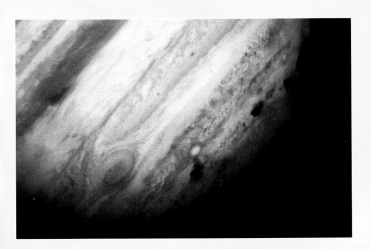

△ *The southern part of Jupiter, photographed in July 1994 by the* Hubble Space Telescope. *Dark chemicals welling up from deep in the atmosphere mark the impact sites of fragments of comet Shoemaker Levy 9. Each mark lasted for several months.*

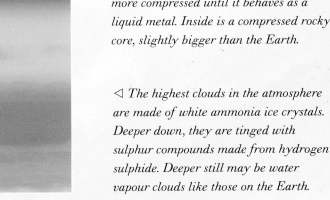

△ *Jupiter's clouds lie in a thin layer on the surface. Below this, the atmosphere of hydrogen and helium becomes more and more compressed until it behaves as a liquid metal. Inside is a compressed rocky core, slightly bigger than the Earth.*

◁ *The highest clouds in the atmosphere are made of white ammonia ice crystals. Deeper down, they are tinged with sulphur compounds made from hydrogen sulphide. Deeper still may be water vapour clouds like those on the Earth.*

Jupiter's Moons

△ *In the shadow of Jupiter lies the frozen world of Europa. A faint greenish light penetrates cracks in the ice. Some scientists think that under the ice there could even be liquid water.*

When Galileo first looked at Jupiter through his telescope in January 1610, he saw three, then four, tiny star-like objects moving close to the planet. He quickly realised that these were moons orbiting Jupiter. Each of these moons – Callisto, Ganymede, Europa and Io – is a world in its own right. We now know of 12 other moons. These include four that orbit inside Galileo's moons. Outside them lie four more, 11 million kilometres from Jupiter. Finally, at twice that distance, are another four. These may have been passing asteroids, captured by Jupiter's gravity.

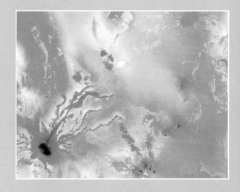

△ *The orange, sulphurous surface of Io is churned up by Jupiter's gravity, resulting in these fresh lava flows from a volcanic crater. The volcanic gases escape into space to form a ring around Jupiter.*

Callisto and Ganymede

Callisto is the same size as Mercury and is covered almost entirely with craters. Its crust is a mixture of ice and rock. One huge impact structure, called Valhalla, consists of rings up to 3,000 km across. Under the dark, dirty surface, the crust may be 300 km deep, with water or slush lying underneath. Ganymede is the largest moon in the Solar System at 5,276 km across. Its icy surface has large, dark patches that are heavily cratered. Ganymede's magnetic field raises the possibility that it still has an active interior.

◁ *The grooved surface of Ganymede appears to be made up of separate slabs of icy material.*

The mystery of Europa

Europa is only 1,525 km across but it could turn out to be the most exciting of all Jupiter's moons. The smooth, white surface has very few craters, but is crazed by numerous cracks. The cracks look very similar to those in pack-ice on the Earth. This suggests that the ice is floating on an ocean of liquid water. Hydrothermal vents in the ocean floor might provide energy as they do on the Earth, and it is just possible that life could have developed in the cold, dark water.

Io, world of fire

Io is the most volcanically active world in the Solar System. It is tugged so hard by Jupiter's gravity that tidal forces churn up the interior, keeping it partly molten. The Voyager craft saw eruptions taking place, with sulphur dioxide spewing 300 km up into space. *Galileo* saw several new volcanoes. Some have left dark lava flows and red and yellow patches of sulphur, making this moon look like a mouldy orange.

△ *This composite picture shows Jupiter dwarfing its four main moons. Closest to the great planet is Io (top), followed by Europa, Ganymede – the largest moon – and Callisto.*

◁ *If oceans do exist beneath Europa's icy surface, there is also the possibility of life flourishing in the cold water. Volcanic vents on the ocean floor could provide the energy to support life, whatever form it might take.*

▷ *Callisto's ancient surface is pockmarked by billions of years of impacts.*

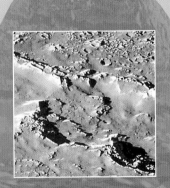

△ Voyager 2 *revealed the cracked, icy surface of Europa. In close-up the structures resemble those found in pack-ice around the Earth's poles, with tilted slabs, cracks and icebergs.*

Saturn

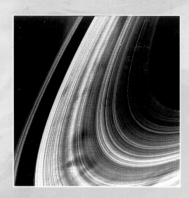

△ Voyager 1 *found dark lines running across Saturn's rings, like spokes on a wheel. Since the rings orbit at different speeds, the spokes were difficult to explain. They are now thought to be caused by ice crystals charged with static electricity.*

After Galileo discovered Jupiter's moons he turned his attention to what appeared to be a triple planet – Saturn. Then the objects to the sides seemed to disappear, making him suspect they were gas clouds. It was the Dutch astronomer Christiaan Huygens who finally realized, in 1675, that Saturn was a ringed planet. Just under two hundred years later it was shown that the rings could not possibly be solid discs, but must be made up of millions of smaller particles of rock or ice, each acting like a tiny moon. When space probes *Pioneer*

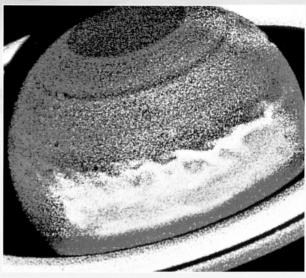

△ *An image, taken by the* Hubble Space Telescope *in 1990, enhanced to show the clouds. An elongated Great White Spot of ammonia ice crystals has formed high up in the atmosphere. The false colours pick out the top of the spot in red.*

11 (1979), *Voyager 1* (1980) and *Voyager 2* (1981) flew past Saturn, it quickly became clear that there are thousands of separate bands of different density within the main rings (which are named A, B, C, D and E). There is also a very thin F ring outside these, its particles kept in line by two tiny moons. The rings are less than 30 metres thick and may have formed from the break-up of a giant comet that strayed too close to Saturn.

△ *As* Voyager 2 *drew away from Saturn, it photographed the rings illuminated from behind. By tracking a star passing behind the rings, thousands of individual ringlets were recorded.*

Stormy weather

A constant dull yellow haze of high ammonia clouds masks most of the deeper structure of Saturn's atmosphere. Occasionally, telescopes can make out a huge, swirling, white storm system. Computer enhancement of the Voyager images revealed circulating bands of cloud similar to Jupiter's. The fastest winds race around Saturn's equator, reaching up to 1,800 kilometres per hour. To the north and south of the equator are alternating bands of slow and fast winds.

▷ *Two pictures of Saturn taken by the* Hubble Space Telescope. *In the top picture, the shadow of the rings and Titan, Saturn's largest moon, are visible. In the bottom picture, Saturn appears with its rings tilted.*

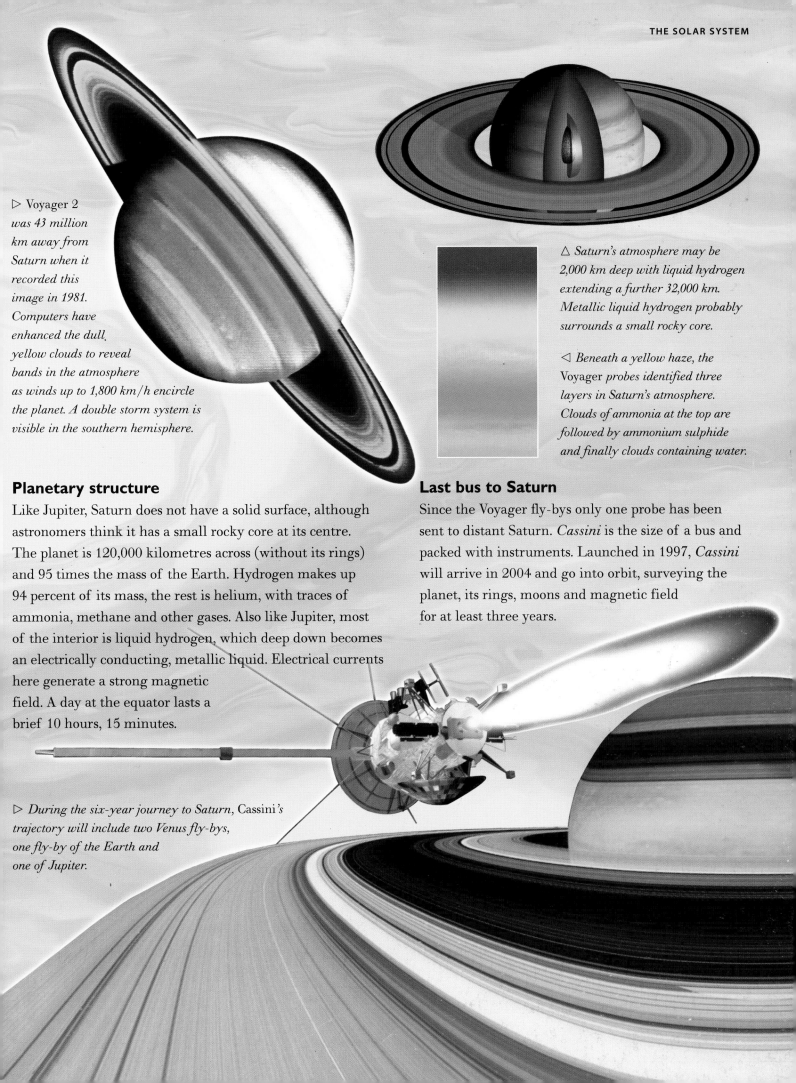

▷ Voyager 2 was 43 million km away from Saturn when it recorded this image in 1981. Computers have enhanced the dull yellow clouds to reveal bands in the atmosphere as winds up to 1,800 km/h encircle the planet. A double storm system is visible in the southern hemisphere.

△ Saturn's atmosphere may be 2,000 km deep with liquid hydrogen extending a further 32,000 km. Metallic liquid hydrogen probably surrounds a small rocky core.

◁ Beneath a yellow haze, the Voyager probes identified three layers in Saturn's atmosphere. Clouds of ammonia at the top are followed by ammonium sulphide and finally clouds containing water.

Planetary structure

Like Jupiter, Saturn does not have a solid surface, although astronomers think it has a small rocky core at its centre. The planet is 120,000 kilometres across (without its rings) and 95 times the mass of the Earth. Hydrogen makes up 94 percent of its mass, the rest is helium, with traces of ammonia, methane and other gases. Also like Jupiter, most of the interior is liquid hydrogen, which deep down becomes an electrically conducting, metallic liquid. Electrical currents here generate a strong magnetic field. A day at the equator lasts a brief 10 hours, 15 minutes.

Last bus to Saturn

Since the Voyager fly-bys only one probe has been sent to distant Saturn. *Cassini* is the size of a bus and packed with instruments. Launched in 1997, *Cassini* will arrive in 2004 and go into orbit, surveying the planet, its rings, moons and magnetic field for at least three years.

▷ During the six-year journey to Saturn, Cassini's trajectory will include two Venus fly-bys, one fly-by of the Earth and one of Jupiter.

Saturn's Moons

Saturn is at the centre of a solar system in miniature. Apart from the billions of particles making up its rings, 23 different moons have been identified. Some are lumps of rock only a few kilometres across that lie close to the planet and shepherd the rings into place. Saturn's most distant moon, Phoebe, is nearly 13 million kilometres from the planet. The biggest of all the moons is Titan. At 5,150 kilometres across, it is bigger than Mercury and has a thick atmosphere. It is the only atmosphere astronomers know of, apart from the Earth's, that is made up mostly of nitrogen. The surface of Titan is very cold (about −180°C) and the atmospheric pressure is double that of our own planet. Titan's atmosphere resembles the early Earth's, but kept in frozen lifelessness.

△ *Discovered by Christiaan Huygens in 1655, Titan is the second largest moon in the Solar System.* Voyager 2 *was only able to see this orange ball of smog, made by the action of sunlight on Titan's atmosphere.*

▽ *High in Titan's nitrogen atmosphere is a layer that absorbs ultraviolet rays. A thin blue haze of carbon chemicals sits above an unbroken layer of orange smog. Below this, the sky may have clouds of methane.*

△ *In November 2004, after a seven year journey, the* Huygens *probe will be released above the clouds of Titan from the* Cassini *Saturn orbiter. After an initial fiery entry, the heat shield will fall away and the probe will parachute down to the surface of the moon.*

A giant among moons

The interior of Titan is probably a mixture of rock and ice, with a rocky core that has an ice mantle. The ice could never melt, but there may be lakes or oceans on Titan, not of water but of liquid natural gas or methane. Methane rain or snow may fall from the clouds. The Voyager probes were unable to see any features on Titan because it is wrapped in a thick, butterscotch yellow, chemical smog.

Mysterious worlds

Saturn's other large moons are equally strange. Enceladus has an ancient, cratered landscape with signs of newer activity in the form of smooth plains and series of ridges. Iapetus, the outermost of Saturn's big moons, is little denser than water, suggesting it is mostly ice. One side is bright and cratered but the opposite side is as black as anything in the Solar System. Dione has light, wispy markings that may be trails of frost sprayed out from ice volcanoes. Mimas, just outside the rings, has an enormous crater, like a great black eye. Tethys is made up mostly of pure ice and has a huge crack, 100 kilometres across and five kilometres deep, running almost pole to pole.

Landing on Titan

On November 27, 2004 the *Cassini* Saturn orbiter will release the *Huygens* probe above the clouds of Titan. No one knows what the probe will find. It may land on rock or ice, or even in a sea of liquid methane. If waves do not sink it, the probe will use sonar to measure depths, as well as recording temperatures and composition. It may even find the basic chemicals needed for life, suspended in a deep freeze.

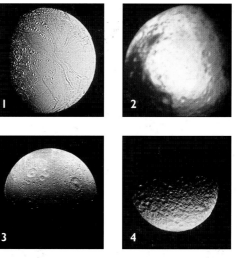

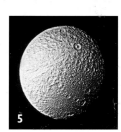

△ *These Voyager images show five of Saturn's large moons: Enceladus (1), Iapetus (2), Dione (3), Mimas (4), and Tethys (5).*

▽ *The* Huygens *probe will have 2.5 hours to make its readings as it descends through the smog of Titan. It is designed to survive landings on both solid and liquid surfaces.*

Uranus

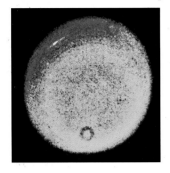

△ *By using computers to stretch blues and greens into a wider spectrum, scientists were able to see white clouds of methane near Uranus' equator* (top left).

Mercury, Venus, Mars, Jupiter and Saturn are all visible to the naked eye and have been known since ancient times. Uranus was the first planet to be discovered through a telescope. One March night in 1781, the astronomer William Herschel noticed what he described as "either a nebulous star or perhaps a comet". He had actually become the first person to discover Uranus. Although it is four times the size of the Earth, Uranus is twice as far away as Saturn and, even through a telescope, only appears as a tiny greenish disc. Herschel wanted to name the new planet after the English king, George III, but in the end it was named after Uranus, the Greek god of the sky.

Cloudy world

Only one probe, *Voyager 2*, has visited Uranus, on January 24, 1986. No one knew what it would find as the planet appears totally featureless through telescopes on the Earth. When the probe's pictures were enhanced they revealed clouds on the surface. These show that the planet rotates once every 17 hours, 14 minutes, with winds blowing at up to 300 kilometres per hour.

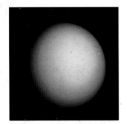

▽ *Combining images taken by* Voyager 2 *through orange, blue and green filters revealed Uranus as a featureless blue ball.*

Surprise discovery

In March 1977, astronomers noticed a star passing behind Uranus. Hoping to record how it dimmed as it disappeared behind the atmosphere, they tracked it with an infrared telescope. To their amazement, the star flickered on and off. The only explanation was that Uranus is encircled by rings.

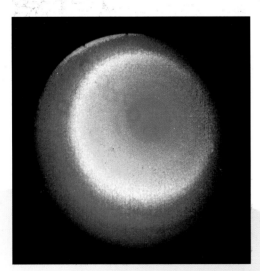

◁ *This colour-enhanced picture, taken as* Voyager 2 *approached Uranus' south pole, indicated that a high altitude haze had formed during the southern hemisphere's 42-year-long summer.*

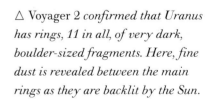

△ Voyager 2 *confirmed that Uranus has rings, 11 in all, of very dark, boulder-sized fragments. Here, fine dust is revealed between the main rings as they are backlit by the Sun.*

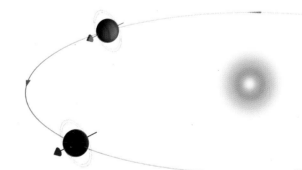

◁ *Miranda, only 480 km across, has a very varied landscape with old, cratered plains and ice cliffs. Regions like the Chevron* (below) *suggest the moon was once almost completely shattered by a major impact.*

Multiple moons

Until the *Voyager 2* mission, Uranus was known to have five moons – Oberon, Titania, Umbriel, Ariel and Miranda (all named after characters from English literature). As *Voyager 2* approached, another moon was spotted and named Puck. A further nine small, dark moons were also found. The two innermost moons, Cordelia and Ophelia, on opposite sides of the outer ring, help shepherd the ring particles into line. One astronomer commented that God must have taken a shaker and scattered moons in all directions.

△ *Three of Uranus' main moons are shown here. Oberon* (1) *has big impact craters, containing dark, carbon-rich material. Ariel* (2) *is covered in places by small craters and resurfaced in others by eruptions of lava or water. Umbriel* (3) *has a dark, cratered surface, but no signs of geological activity.*

◁ *The atmosphere of Uranus is made up of hydrogen, helium and a small percentage of methane. It has very few cloud markings.*

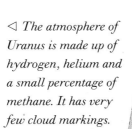

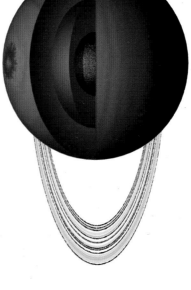

◁ *Uranus probably has a rocky core with a mantle of ammonia, methane and water ice that may be partially liquid.*

△ *The blue-green gas giant Uranus is four times the size of the Earth. It has a strange magnetic field aligned at 60° to the rotation axis and off-centred 10,000 km from the heart of the planet. It may be generated by electrical currents in the watery mantle.*

Strange rotation

Unlike the other planets, Uranus' axis of rotation is at right angles to its orbit around the Sun. So, as *Voyager 2* approached Uranus' south pole, the rings and moons seemed to circle the planet like a target. This also gives Uranus very strange seasons. The poles are the warmest places on the planet. The south pole has a summer lasting 42 years, when the Sun never sets, while the opposite pole is plunged into total darkness for 42 years.

◁ *Uranus rotates at an angle of 97° to the Sun during its 84-year orbit.*

▷ *The orbits of Uranus' five main moons are shown here. From the outside in they are: Oberon, Titania, Umbriel, Ariel and Miranda. They orbit in circular paths in the same direction as the planet's rotation.*

Neptune

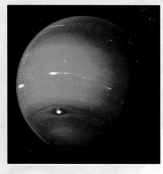

After the discovery of Uranus, astronomers were unable to make sense of its orbit around the Sun – it seemed as if something was pulling it off course. In 1845, Cambridge graduate John Couch Adams proposed this movement was being caused by an eighth planet, and a year later his professor, James Challis, began a search. In France, Urbain Leverrier had made similar predictions and, although Challis had seen the new planet without recognizing it, Berlin astronomers using the French predictions actually made the discovery of Neptune

△ This image, made by Voyager 2 in 1989, has been enhanced to reveal a haze high in the atmosphere and white clouds of methane ice.

in 1846. They named the blue-green planet after the Roman god of the sea. It is 4.5 billion kilometres from the Sun and takes 165 years to orbit it (a Neptunian year).

◁ The Great Dark Spot, fringed with methane ice clouds, is as big as the Earth. It travels around Neptune backwards. The Solar System's fastest winds blow around it at 2,000 km/h.

△ Neptune is made up of a thick mantle of liquid water and gases around a rocky core. It has a magnetic field inclined at 50° to its axis and 10,000 km off-centre. It has rings made up of large particles and broad bands of finer dust.

Weather forecast

Neptune's atmosphere consists of 85 percent hydrogen, thirteen percent helium and two percent methane. It is bitterly cold (the cloud tops are −210°C) but heat is produced in the interior. Neptune is a very active planet. Clouds of methane rise through the atmosphere and violent winds blow at over 1,000 kilometres per hour. One cloud pattern, the Scooter, speeds around the planet passing another feature, the Great Dark Spot, every few days.

△ The atmosphere is topped by a thin haze with cirrus clouds of methane ice. Sunlight causes reactions in the methane, producing hydrocarbon snow. As this falls, it reverts to methane gas and rises again.

◁ High-speed winds have stretched out these high cirrus clouds of methane into streamers. They cast shadows onto the blue main cloud deck, 50 km below.

◁ *Neptune's two main moons, Triton and Nereid, have very different orbits. Nereid's long elliptical orbit lasts 360 days. Triton's 5.9-day orbit circles the planet backwards. Both may have been caught by Neptune's gravity as they passed.*

Rings and moons

Before *Voyager 2*'s fly-past of Neptune in 1989, only two moons and partial rings were known to astronomers. The craft's cameras confirmed complete rings, bands of dust and six new moons. The largest of these is Proteus. It is 436 kilometres across and has a giant 150-kilometre crater. Next in size is Larissa at 208 kilometres. The other four moons lie between the rings. The outermost moon, Nereid, may be a captured comet. Neptune's largest moon, Triton, is 2,706 kilometres across. With no high mountains and few craters, its surface may have been flooded by eruptions of liquid water and ammonia. Most of its surface is ice, but the poles are capped with a pink snow of frozen nitrogen.

▽ *Triton's south pole is capped by a light, pinkish substance that is probably frozen nitrogen accumulated during its long winter in shadow. The grooved and wrinkled surface to the north has a red tint, possibly due to hydrocarbons produced by the action of sunlight.*

△ *This imagined view from the surface of Triton shows Neptune on the horizon and an active nitrogen geyser erupting from the surface. Pressure keeps nitrogen liquid deep below the ground.* *As it rises it explodes as a mixture of ice crystals and vapour. The eruption carries the plume 30 km high, before it blows away in the thin wind, raining a dark streak of dust down onto the surface.*

Pluto

In order to explain the orbit of Uranus, astronomers realized they had to discover something else. An American astronomer, Percival Lowell, predicted a planet larger than the Earth and searched for it in vain (Pluto appeared on his photographs, but he failed to recognize it). However, Clyde Tombaugh, a successor at the observatory Lowell founded in Arizona, USA, painstakingly compared star after star and, finally found an object that moved. Named Pluto (after the Greek god of the underworld) at the suggestion of an eleven-year-old girl, it is six billion kilometres from the Sun and one four-hundredth the mass of the Earth.

△ *This image of Pluto is made up from measurements taken by the* Hubble Space Telescope. *The lightest patches may be nitrogen ice.*

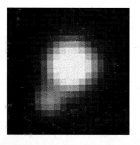

△ *Even the most powerful Earth-based telescopes can only just make out the faint disc of Pluto and its moon, Charon. No probe has visited Pluto and there is still much to learn about it.*

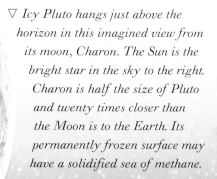

△ *Pluto is usually the furthest planet from the Sun, but its elliptical orbit* (orange) *briefly brings it closer than* Neptune (blue). *Some astronomers suggest that a Planet X* (green) *follows a steeply inclined orbit far outside Pluto. The Kuiper Belt – a ring of small, icy objects lies beyond the planets.*

▽ *Icy Pluto hangs just above the horizon in this imagined view from its moon, Charon. The Sun is the bright star in the sky to the right. Charon is half the size of Pluto and twenty times closer than the Moon is to the Earth. Its permanently frozen surface may have a solidified sea of methane.*

Seeing double

When it was first discovered, Pluto's mass and density were unknown, so no one knew if it was the final explanation for the outer planets' orbits. If Pluto had a moon, however, the masses could be calculated from that moon's orbit. There the matter rested until 1978, when Jim Christy was trying to make precise measurements of Pluto at the US Naval Observatory. At first, his picture seemed pear-shaped. Suddenly, he realized he was seeing not one object but two. He named the moon Charon after his wife, and also after the mythological ferryman of the ancient Greek underworld.

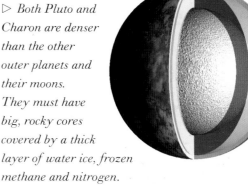

▷ *Both Pluto and Charon are denser than the other outer planets and their moons. They must have big, rocky cores covered by a thick layer of water ice, frozen methane and nitrogen.*

△ *This picture taken by the* Hubble Space Telescope *shows Pluto and Charon. Pluto at 2,300 km across is far smaller than our Moon, while Charon is less than 1,200 km across.*

◁ *A faint line among the points of stars reveals an object in the Kuiper Belt. Only a few kilometres across, a few hundred of these objects have been observed with powerful infrared telescopes.*

Planet X and beyond

Pluto, however, did not account for all the discrepancies in Uranus' orbit and astonomers started searching for a tenth planet, Planet X. Clyde Tombaugh searched for 13 years, plotting the positions of 45 million stars and identifying 775 asteroids in the process. Some people predicted that a planet would be found in an orbit angled to the other planets, while others thought that the Sun has a distant, dark companion. There may also be billions of comets beyond the planets, all adding their own gravitational effect. A belt of icy objects has been discovered far beyond Pluto, known as the Kuiper Belt. Each object is only a few kilometres across and may be the frozen left-overs from planetary formation.

△ *Pluto has a thin atmosphere of nitrogen and methane. This thickens as the planet's elliptical orbit brings it nearer the Sun and warms it up. Polar caps of methane ice may be deposited as Pluto cools again.*

Comets

Comets are among the most beautiful and exciting sights in the sky. They are made all the more mysterious by their unpredictability, leading people in the past to think that they were omens of either good or evil. Five hundred years ago, they were thought to be within our atmosphere. Then, in 1577, Danish astronomer Tycho Brahe worked out the distance to a comet and showed that they came from beyond the planets, and rounded the Sun before returning to deep space. We now know that there must be a vast number of comets in the outer regions of the Solar System, far beyond the planets. In fact, there could be billions waiting in the deep-freeze of space.

△ *This engraving from the* Nuremberg Chronicle *(published in 1493) depicts the sighting of Halley's Comet in* AD684.

△ *In the* Adoration of the Magi *by Giotto, Halley's Comet is shown as the Star of Bethlehem, above the stable.*

Halley's Comet

Edmond Halley (1656–1742) studied the records of comets and realized that the comets of 1531, 1607 and 1682 were actually the same object. He predicted correctly the comet's return in 1759, although he never lived to see it. In fact, Halley's Comet has been seen 30 times since 240BC. It is depicted in the Bayeux Tapestry, which shows the Norman Conquest of England in 1066, and in a painting of the Nativity by the Italian artist Giotto, based on his sighting of the comet in 1301. In 1986, a probe named *Giotto* visited Halley's Comet.

△ *This computer simulation shows how the front dust shield of Giotto looked after speeding past the nucleus of Halley's Comet. Dust particles punched holes in the metal. Giotto took a close-up picture of the comet's dark nucleus (right) silhouetted against brighter jets of gas.*

▽ *In 1997, Comet Hale-Bopp gave a great display. Its nucleus was unusually large and it started to brighten beyond Jupiter's orbit.*

△ *This image of Comet Hale-Bopp, taken in 1996, is coloured to show the bright coma as well as the dark nucleus embedded deep within it.*

The core of a comet

Comets are all show and very little substance. The head of a comet is made up of a small nucleus, only a few kilometres across. It may contain lumps of rock, but they are loosely bound by ice and comets often break up. As the nucleus approaches the inner Solar System, ice begins to vaporize, creating the bright coma (a sphere of gas and dust around the nucleus), and tail, which can be millions of kilometres long. A crust of black, carbon-rich material covers the surface with jets of gas breaking out through cracks. Each time a comet passes the Sun it loses millions of tonnes of ice, eventually leaving a dead, dark nucleus or just a trail of dust.

▽ *The nucleus of a comet is like a huge, dirty snowball. Jets of gas and dust escape through fissures in its black, asphalt-like surface, blown by the solar wind to form a tail. Here, the surface has been cut away to reveal the icy interior, surrounding a loosely-bound, rocky core.*

△ *Comets have two tails. Electrically charged ions of gas always point directly away from the Sun. The yellower dust tail lags slightly and curves with the comet's motion.*

Dead comets and shooting stars

Long after a comet has run out of bright gas and faded for good, anything that is left of the nucleus, along with a stream of dusty particles, continues in the same orbit. When the Earth passes through this orbit, thousands of the particles burn up as shooting stars in the atmosphere. These are the meteor showers that seem to radiate out from the same place in the sky at the same time each year. Spectacular storms look as if they emerge from particular constellations. For example, the Perseid shower, which follows Comet Swift-Tuttle, appears from the constellation Perseus, while the Orionids, which follow Halley's Comet, seem to come from Orion.

△ *Blown back by the solar wind (a constant stream of electrically charged particles emitted by the Sun), a comet's tails always point away from the Sun. The tails are longest closest to the Sun, when gas production is at its highest.*

The Oort Cloud

Far out, on the edge of the Solar System, lies a gigantic cloud of billions of frozen comets, called the Oort Cloud. Some comets are concentrated in a disc beyond the orbit of Pluto, while others are randomly distributed up to a light year or more away. The gravity of nearby stars 'knocks' these comets from their orbits so that they fall towards the Sun. About ten comets a year are newcomers to the inner Solar System, where many become trapped. The Oort Cloud may be debris left over from when the Solar System formed. If so, comets may be able to tell us what conditions were like when the Sun was born.

△ *An exposure of only a few seconds captured the bright streaks of the Leonid meteor shower, which seems to radiate from the constellation Leo and follows Comet Tempel-Tuttle.*

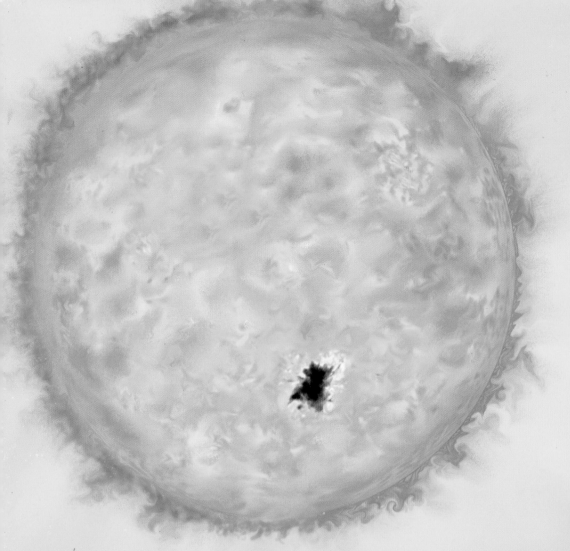

△ *The Sun has been burning for about five billion years. Like all stars, it is a huge ball of very hot gas. Its constant stream of sunshine keeps our planet warm, enables plants to photosynthesize and ultimately sustains all life.*

▽ *During a total eclipse, the corona — the outer layer of the Sun's atmosphere — becomes visible. It can reach temperatures of up to 2,000,000°C.*

The Active Sun

△ *Sunlight scatters off dust and clouds in the Earth's atmosphere to produce spectacular sunrises and sunsets.*

The Sun is our nearest star, the centre of the Solar System and the source, directly or indirectly, of almost all the energy we use. The Sun is extremely hot — about 6,000°C at the surface, or photosphere, and 15,000,000°C at the core. The core temperature and pressure are high enough for an energy-generating process called nuclear fusion to take place. Protons, the nuclei of hydrogen atoms, fuse together to make deuterium or heavy hydrogen, then helium. At each stage, mass is lost in the form of energy. Altogether the Sun loses four million tonnes of mass every second, which is converted into the four hundred billion billion megawatts of energy it needs to support itself and to shine. Most of the energy radiates as heat, light and gamma rays, taking thousands of years to reach the surface. But some escapes straight through the Sun, carried by ghostly particles called neutrinos, produced in the nuclear reactions.

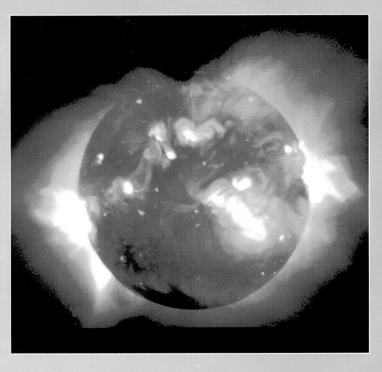

△ *This x-ray image of the Sun and its corona was recorded by the Japanese satellite* Yohkoh *in 1992. The brightest and hottest areas occur above sunspots, where hot gases flare up.*

Eclipse!

About once a year, the Moon comes between the Sun and the Earth, casting a shadow. When the Moon is close enough to the Earth in its orbit, it masks the Sun's disc entirely, causing a total eclipse.

▽ *During a total eclipse, part of the world is plunged into darkness. People in the outer shadow see a partial eclipse.*

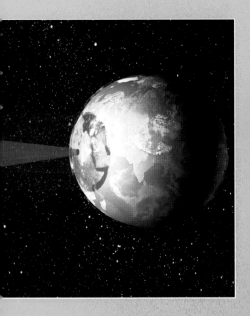

▷ *Nuclear reactions take place inside the core of the Sun and the energy slowly radiates out to a distance of about 600,000 kilometres. Huge bubbles of hot gas continue the transfer of energy to the surface.*

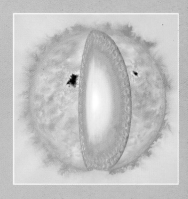

Observing the Sun

You should not look at the Sun directly and certainly never through a telescope or binoculars – you risk being blinded for life. It is possible, however, to project an image onto a sheet of paper using binoculars, a lens or even a pinhole in a sheet of cardboard. This is essentially what solar astronomers do, focusing the light down long tubes, through filters and onto an observation table.

Unobstructed view

The Sun is best viewed from beyond our turbulent atmosphere. From space the Sun can be seen in other wavelengths such as x-rays, revealing the superhot flares that leap from the surface. Several spacecraft have studied the Sun directly, including *Skylab* in the 1970s and *SolarMax* in the 1980s. *Ulysses* has left the plane of the planets to study the magnetic field and solar wind above the poles of the Sun. And Europe's *SOHO* craft hangs between the Earth and the Sun looking at sunquakes and flares, and spotting storms of particles on their way to the Earth.

△ *The Sun is ringing like a bell. Scientists can record the vibrations by seeing how the movement stretches or compresses light from different regions. The sound waves are created in the solar convective zone – the outer layer of the Sun.*

△ *The McMath Solar Telescope on Kitt Peak in Arizona, focuses the Sun's image down a 152 m diagonal tube to instruments below.*

Outside the Sun

The hot, electrically-charged gas within the Sun generates very powerful magnetic fields. Where these break the surface, great jets or loops of hot gas called prominences lift off into space. Dark, relatively cool patches on the Sun's surface are called sunspots. These form in pairs or groups, and represent points where the magnetic field lines leave and re-join the surface. Rapid eruptions called solar flares also arise along these lines. They usually last no longer than ten minutes and release the energy equivalent of a million hydrogen bombs. Together with the solar wind (a constant stream of charged particles flowing from the Sun), they create a vast envelope, known as the heliosphere, around the Solar System.

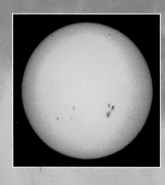

△ *A visible light image of the Sun, taken with the McMath Solar Telescope in Arizona. Several sunspots can clearly be seen on the photosphere, or the visible surface of the Sun.*

△ *Prominences of hot gas break free from the Sun's surface and can leap out hundreds of thousands of kilometres into space.*

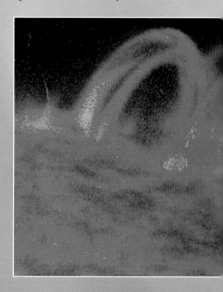

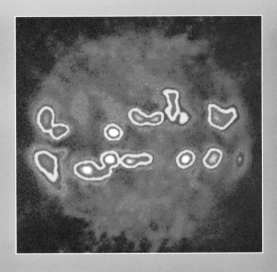

△ *The Sun emits strong radio waves that were first noticed in the 1940s. The brightest areas in this radio image occur where gas flares off into space above pairs of sunspots.*

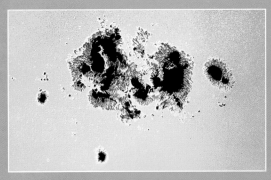

△ *This false-colour photograph shows a group of sunspots. The spots form in pairs with opposite magnetic poles. The dark centres of the spots are the coolest, lowest regions where strong magnetic fields slow the upward flow of heat. Around them, bubbles of gas rise, cool and move away.*

The changing Sun

The Sun is not as constant as it appears. By tracking sunspots, it is clear that it rotates at the equator once every 25 days, and at the poles once every 35 days. This difference results in magnetic field lines getting wrapped around the Sun until they break through the surface at sunspots. The pattern of sunspots changes in a cycle of about 11 years. At the start, spots begin to appear near the poles. As they fade, spots appear nearer and nearer the equator, where they cause a peak of solar activity.

◁ *Magnetic field lines snake out from a sunspot with north polarity and re-enter a spot with south polarity. The magnetic lines form tubes along which hot gas flows.*

Solar weather

There are less dramatic changes, too. Between 1645 and 1715, there were virtually no sunspots. It coincided with extreme winters in Europe, a period sometimes known as the 'Little Ice Age'. Evidence from other Sun-like stars suggests that, for up to 20 percent of their time, they have no sunspots.

◁ *These great loops of hot gas were photographed in ultraviolet by Skylab in 1973. They arch up between pairs of sunspots and can remain relatively stable for many hours or even days.*

The end of the Sun

It probably took the Sun 3.5 billion years to reach its present brightness, during which time plants were slowly using up carbon dioxide from the Earth's atmosphere, reducing the greenhouse effect and keeping the climate more or less constant. The Sun will probably continue to shine at its present level for another two billion years. But in about six billion years' time, hydrogen will begin to run out at the core, and the Sun will begin to expand rapidly and cool as it becomes a dying star called a red giant. This will engulf the inner planets, including the Earth.

△ *In about six billion years' time, the Earth's atmosphere and oceans will boil away as the dying Sun becomes a red giant. As the giant star expands, the baked husk of our planet will be swallowed up and become part of a new generation of stars and planets.*

▽ Swirling nebulae of dust and gas are the nurseries of stars. Often, they are themselves the ashes of earlier generations, cooked and spewed out from short-lived massive stars.

Star Birth

△ Knots form in the gas as gravity pulls it together. As the gas compresses it begins to heat up.

The backdrop of stars used to be thought of as constant and unchanging. Over human lifetimes, there is little detectable change, but over the billions of years of galactic life, stars are born, live their lives, grow old and die. Space, by human standards, appears very, very empty. But collect together all the gas and dust of supposedly empty space and there is more matter than all the stars and planets put together. It is out of these clouds, or nebulae, that new stars are born. Over 12 billion years ago, when the Universe itself was young, clouds of hydrogen and helium created the first stars that ever shone. Now, all kinds of other elements are mixed in, the ashes of earlier generations of stars. These combine to make the stars we see forming in dusty nebulae today.

△ Below the line of three stars that form the belt of Orion is Orion's Sword. At its centre lies the distinctive Orion Nebula, a birthplace of stars.

Conception!

Stars tend to be born not singly but in nurseries, where sufficiently dense clouds of gas have accumulated. Star formation can be triggered simply by the gravitational pull of the gas, or when a shock wave passes through it from, for example, a nearby exploding star or intergalactic collision.

▷ Altogether, 700 young stars have been spotted in the dust and gas clouds of the Orion Nebula, illuminated here by visible and ultraviolet light.

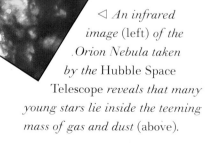

◁ An infrared image (left) of the Orion Nebula taken by the Hubble Space Telescope reveals that many young stars lie inside the teeming mass of gas and dust (above).

△ *The gas begins to spiral around in a disc. The protostar expels jets of gas from its poles.*

△ *Nuclear fusion begins in the hot core. Gas is expelled in a wind that blows the dust away.*

△ *Finally, the star begins to shine steadily.*

Getting warm

As knots of gas inside the cloud become compressed, they begin to warm up. This contraction causes the cloud to rotate faster, making the gas form into a disc. Matter falling inwards from the disc is ejected in jets from the poles. Eventually the central protostar becomes so hot and compressed that the process of nuclear fusion begins at its core. This in turn causes more material to be blown off and, finally, the remains of the disc blow away – apart from any lumps that are forming into planets – and the new star shines into clear space.

Seeing cool, seeing deep

At the different stages of a star's birth and life-cycle, matter glows with different wavelengths. When stars begin to form, warm gas radiates in infrared wavelengths, while cooler dust and molecules glow at sub-millimetre radio wavelengths. Infrared and radio waves can also penetrate the thick clouds, so it is at these wavelengths that astronomers peer into the nebulae and watch stars being born.

△ *Baby stars hatch from EGGs (Evaporating Gaseous Globules), the finger-like tips emerging from this pillar of gas in the Eagle Nebula. This picture was taken by the* Hubble Space Telescope.

▷ *The* Hubble Space Telescope *has revealed more than 150 of these disc-like knots in the Orion Nebula. They provide the best evidence so far that planetary systems can form at the same time as stars.*

Star Life

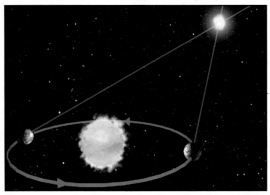

Stars come in all sizes and colours. Look up on a clear, dark, night and you will see hundreds, perhaps thousands of stars. Look with a powerful telescope and you will see millions, perhaps even billions. Some are bright, others faint. Some look blue, others white, yellow or red. There are stars that are bright simply because they are nearby. Certain stars are, in absolute terms, hundreds of times brighter than the Sun, others thousands of times dimmer. A star's colour reflects its surface temperature. Blue stars are very hot, while red ones are cooler. Their ages vary as well. Some are almost as old as the Universe, others are babies in comparison. It is the smaller stars that live longest. Big stars burn up their nuclear fuel much faster and only last a few million years.

△ As the Earth moves in its orbit around the Sun, nearby stars appear to move against the distant background. This displacement is called parallax, and it is used to measure the distances to stars.

The main sequence

Most stars follow a fixed relationship between their temperature and brightness. They begin as red dwarfs and become hotter and brighter. This period of a star's life – when it is shining almost constantly – is known as the 'main sequence'. How long it lasts depends on the star's mass. When the hydrogen burning in its core runs out, the star expands and cools into a red giant, leaving the main sequence. Eventually the star sheds its outer layers, leaving a slowly cooling white dwarf.

▷ Hipparcos, *the European satellite, has measured the precise position of more than 120,000 stars. It found that some are closer than we previously thought.*

△ The Pleiades open cluster of stars is sometimes known as the Seven Sisters, after the seven bright stars clearly visible to the naked eye. This cluster contains, in fact, almost 500 young, blue stars.

How far to the stars

To find out how bright a star really is, you need to know how far away it is. The brightest star in the sky, Sirius, is quite close (8.6 light years) and, although it is in reality 26 times brighter than the Sun, it is not nearly as bright as some more distant stars. A nearby star's distance can be calculated by measuring its position twice, six months apart, when the Earth is on opposite sides of the Sun. You can see how this works by moving your head from side to side. Objects close to you seem to move against the background. This shift – known as parallax – can be used to calculate the object's distance. Similarly, the apparent motion of stars (caused by the Earth's orbit against the distant background) gives a measure of distance.

A sense of scale

The distances to the stars is vast. Proxima Centuri, the nearest, is 40,000 billion kilometres away, while others are hundreds of times further. Clearly, kilometres are not very convenient units at such scales. Instead, astronomers use light years – a measurement of distance not of time. One light year is the distance light travels in one year. Proxima Centuri is 4.2 light years away, distant indeed.

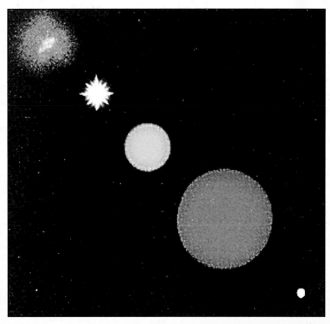

△ *The life story of a star like the Sun begins in a cloud of gas from which a bright, young protostar condenses. For eight billion years it shines as a yellow star, then expands into a red giant before becoming a white dwarf.*

Variable stars

Some stars appear to vary in their brightness, either erratically or in a regular cycle. Sometimes it is because they are in binary pairs and one eclipses the other. Young and unstable stars flare out great masses of hot gas into space, while old, red, supergiants send out black sooty clouds of carbon. Others pulsate regularly. One type, the Cepheid variables, alternately inflates and contracts, brightening and fading at a rate directly related to its overall brightness. This makes these stars useful for measuring distances in the Universe.

△ *Sirius* (top) *in the constellation Canis Major is the brightest star in the sky. Sometimes known as the Dog Star, it is part of a binary pair. Its companion star is a faint white dwarf.*

Pairs and clusters

Our Sun shines alone in space, but most stars are members of groups. Frequently, they are in pairs known as binaries. Some are in less stable groups of three, or in double binaries of four. Stars turn up in larger groups too, such as the Pleiades. Some of the closest-packed groups of stars, called globular clusters, may contain millions of stars, light months rather than light years apart.

▷ *This globular cluster in our neighbouring galaxy, Andromeda, has at least 300,000 stars. From the amount of helium that has built up, astronomers have estimated that the stars are almost as old as the Universe itself.*

Star Death

Stars the size of our Sun swell up as hydrogen runs low in their core and they shed layers of gas to form what are known as planetary nebulae. Left behind at the centre is a white dwarf star, which slowly cools to a cinder over billions of years. Bigger stars live briefer, more violent lives. Within them, a constant battle rages between the crushing force of gravity and the outward pressure of heat. If a star's mass is more than 40 percent greater than that of the Sun, not even electrons can hold it up when its nuclear fuel runs out. Electrons in the core become squashed so hard that they fuse with protons to make neutrons. The resulting matter has a density of 300 million tonnes per cubic centimetre and forms a star no bigger than a city, but weighing more than the Sun. The energy released as the core collapses tears through the outer layers of the dying star in a huge supernova explosion.

△ *The Egg Nebula consists of concentric shells of gas ejected by a red giant star near the end of its life. The 'searchlights' are areas where light and jets of particles penetrate gaps in the swirling clouds of dust.*

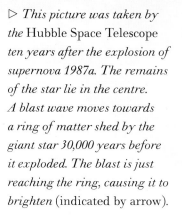

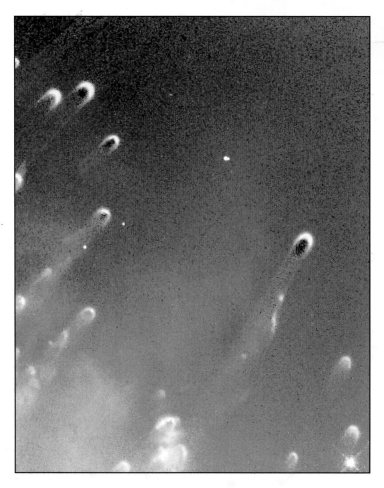

△ *Tadpole-like knots of material in the Helix Planetary Nebula plough into gases ejected earlier from a dying star. Each knot is larger than our own Solar System.*

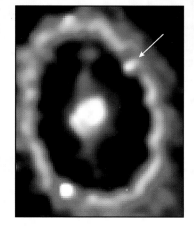

▷ *This picture was taken by the* Hubble Space Telescope *ten years after the explosion of supernova 1987a. The remains of the star lie in the centre. A blast wave moves towards a ring of matter shed by the giant star 30,000 years before it exploded. The blast is just reaching the ring, causing it to brighten* (indicated by arrow).

Going supernova

On February 23, 1987, Canadian astronomer Ian Shelton was making routine observations using a telescope in Chile when he noticed a very bright star which he did not remember seeing before. He soon realized that he had spotted an exploding star, a supernova lying 170,000 light years away. A few hours earlier, special underground detectors in the United States and Japan had picked up a pulse of ghostly neutrinos, particles created when the iron core of a giant star collapses and a neutron star forms. The process had caused a tremendous explosion that tore the star apart in a blaze of hot new radioactive elements.

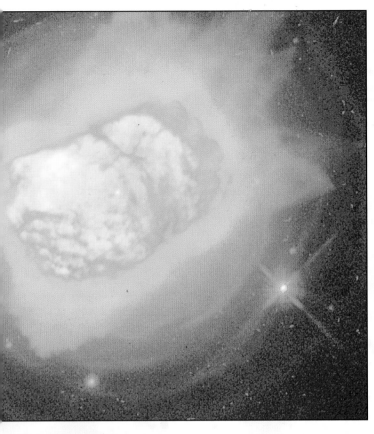

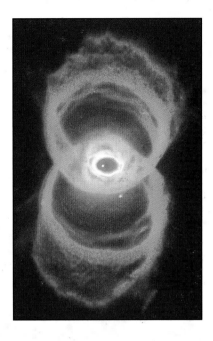

◁ *When the star NGC 7027 swelled into a red giant, it started to shed gas and formed the blue, spherical shell. As the process became more violent, it produced the red and yellow material.*

▷ *The Hourglass Nebula has formed around a star reaching the end of its life. A stellar wind has blown out from the poles creating the double ring.*

The stars, our ancestors

The first matter in the Universe was almost all helium and hydrogen. All the other elements around us today, including carbon, silicon, oxygen, and nitrogen were cooked up in the nuclear furnaces of stars, scattered into space and reformed into solar systems such as ours. All elements that are heavier than iron were created and spewed out in supernova explosions. Our world and even our bodies are made, quite literally, of stardust.

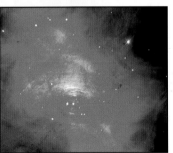

◁ *The Crab Nebula is the remnant of a star that exploded in AD1054. At its centre is a tiny, superdense neutron star, pulsing as it spins thirty times a second and ejecting particles that interact with the gas.*

Pulsars

Every year, several supernova explosions are spotted in distant galaxies and there is plenty of evidence for past explosions nearer home. In AD1054, Chinese astronomers recorded a bright new star, or nova, in the direction of the constellation of Taurus. Today, it is still visible as the Crab Nebula, a bright, expanding shell of radioactive gas and debris. At its centre is a small white star sending out radio pulses thirty times a second. When it was discovered in 1965, it was given the name LGM1 (L for little, G for green and M for man). But this is no alien distress beacon. It is a pulsar, an ultra-dense neutron star, flashing a beam of light and radio waves as it spins. Hundreds have been found since, some spinning up to a thousand times a second.

△ *The bright ray of a pulsar sweeps across space as a neutron star spins on its axis. Escaping electrons are funnelled by the intense magnetic field, sending out a radio beam and light.*

◁ "Oh my ears and whiskers, how late it's getting!" At least both Alice and the White Rabbit agree what time it is as Alice sets out on a journey into a black hole.

Black Hole!

While some dying stars turn into superdense neutron stars, others collapse even further. In a star that is more than three times the Sun's mass, gravity violently crushes matter inwards. It continues to collapse before disappearing into an incredibly dense but dimensionless point called a singularity. A black hole is the space around a singularity, and nothing that falls in can ever go fast enough to escape – not even light. Black holes vary in size – the more massive the singularity, the wider the black hole.

Time for a change

A black hole plays strange tricks on the fabric of space and time, curving it in on itself. If you were able to watch someone falling towards a black hole's outer edge, or event horizon, you would see their clock running slower and slower. At the same time, they would become redder and redder until they faded from view.

The long stretch

If you were the unfortunate person falling in to a black hole, your clock would seem to tick normally and you would remain your usual colour. But you would have other things to worry about. The gravity would pull so hard that it would stretch you out like spaghetti. Your remains would rapidly spiral in, like water down a cosmic plug-hole, and friction would heat them up until they gave off x-rays.

△ Gas is dragged off a massive star (above right) and spirals violently into a black hole. The spinning disc of gas heats up until it emits x-rays and a jet of matter shoots from the poles.

▷ *The gravitational well of a black hole or even a massive star distorts the fabric of space-time. A ray of light travelling from a star to the Earth is bent as it shines past, changing the apparent position of the star.*

▽ *As Alice gets close to the black hole, its gravity begins to act more on her feet than her head and she starts to stretch. It also stretches the light, and her feet grow redder. Alice notices no change in the rate her watch ticks, but already the Rabbit sees her watch running slow.*

Hunting the invisible

Although astronomers cannot see black holes directly they can detect them through their effects. Stars often come in pairs and if one of the pair has collapsed into a black hole it may also pull in gas from the companion star. As the gas spirals in, it emits x-rays. By looking at these x-ray sources, astronomers can study the invisible black hole.

▽ *In what to Alice are the next few seconds, she will be beyond the point of no return – the event horizon. Meanwhile, the Rabbit is getting later and later.*

▷ *Now Alice has really got problems. She becomes 'spaghettified' as the gravitational forces begin to pull her apart. Compared to the Rabbit's watch, her time is running slower and slower.*

The great escape

Although you could never escape from a black hole, something does emerge from them. Pairs of particles, created on the event horizon itself, end up with one falling in, one coming out. The loss of energy is known as 'Hawking radiation'. It is so faint, however, that it would take a hundred billion billion billion billion billion billion years for a black hole with the mass of our Sun to evaporate.

The Milky Way

We have seen how ideas have changed from the ancient notion of our Earth at the centre of the Universe to one where the Sun rules the planets. Today, we know that the Sun is just one among about 200 billion stars in the great star city of our galaxy, the Milky Way. This spiral galaxy is like a vast disc with a bulge in the middle (a bit like two fried eggs, put back to back), with great arms of stars. About three-quarters of the way out along the Orion Arm is our local star, the Sun.

△ *This fish-eye view of the entire night sky above Australia is dominated by the billions of stars that make up the Milky Way.*

The Milky Way is about 100,000 light years across and rotates in space, spinning fastest at its centre (the Solar System is only about 12 light hours across).

Highway of stars

Look up at the sky on a clear, dark night, away from city lights and you can see the great highway of stars that is the Milky Way. It is densest towards its centre, in the constellation of Sagittarius. You will see nearby bright stars, clusters of stars and a faint haze of millions of distant stars. The darker patches that look like holes are really great clouds of dust. The faint remains of ancient supernova explosions show up as a wispy structure of gas all around.

△ *This near-infrared view of the Milky Way clearly shows the central bulge of the Galaxy from our edge-on position within it.*

Among the crowd

We cannot see the centre of the Galaxy (it is shrouded in gas and dust), but infrared and radio waves can penetrate the clouds, giving hints of violent processes at work. It is a very crowded place, with millions of stars and immense quantities of gas. There is a bar-like structure and clouds of molecules. Strong magnetic fields have drawn out gas into thin filaments and a fountain of antimatter rises thousands of light years from the galactic plane.

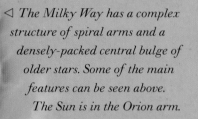

CYGNUS ARM
PERSEUS ARM
CENTRAL BULGE
ORION ARM
SAGGITARIUS ARM
CRUX-CENTAURUS ARM

◁ *The Milky Way has a complex structure of spiral arms and a densely-packed central bulge of older stars. Some of the main features can be seen above. The Sun is in the Orion arm.*

△ *Infrared telescopes can see through the clouds of dust and give a tantalizing glimpse of the Milky Way's centre, where a black hole may lurk.*

Shifting heart

Three hundred light years from the Galaxy's core lies a gamma ray source called the Great Annihilator. Once thought to be the centre of the Milky Way, it produces jets of antimatter and emits gamma rays. It is probably a black hole. The true centre is now known to be Sagittarius A*. This may be a monster black hole more than a million times the mass of the Sun. But if it is, the beast at the centre of the Galaxy appears to be sleeping right now.

1

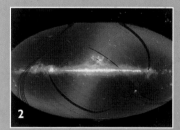

2

△ *The 73 cm wavelength radio map* (1) *reveals high-velocity electrons moving in a magnetic field. It helps astronomers to plot the magnetic field of the Galaxy. The infrared map* (2) *is especially bright where there are*

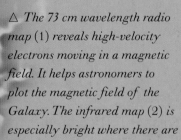

3

dust clouds warmed by hot, new stars. The blue 'S' is dust in our Solar System. The 21 cm radio map (3) *shows up atomic hydrogen in gas clouds between stars. The gas emits a very precise frequency, helping scientists trace its motion in the rotating galaxy.*

Our Local Group

The Milky Way and the Andromeda galaxy are immense spirals of stars, island universes in their own right. They are the two largest and most important members of the Local Group, a cluster of galaxies stretching five million light years across space. The Local Group contains some thirty galaxies, loosely bound together in each other's gravitational pull. Andromeda, which has twice as many stars as our own galaxy, is situated near another small spiral. The other members of the group are smaller still and are either irregular blobs of stars, like the Magellanic clouds near our own spiral galaxy, or are dwarf galaxies.

Cannibal galaxies

It appears that over billions of years, the big spirals, including our own Milky Way, have grown by eating up their neighbours. Some of the nearby dwarf galaxies will be gobbled up by our galaxy in a few million years time. And even the great spiral Andromeda galaxy itself is coming towards our own galaxy at about 300 kilometres every second. It still has a long way to go, but eventually the two galaxies may pass through one another or even merge. The distances between stars are so immense that few will collide, but great clouds of gas and dust might be stirred up into star formation.

▽ In 1912, Henrietta Leavitt discovered that stars called Cepheid variables change their brightness in a predictable way.

▽ The Virgo cluster contains more than 1,000 galaxies. Virgo is over 50 million light years away and is the centre of our supercluster.

△ Henrietta Leavitt

△ Virgo cluster

△ Cepheid star (dim)

△ Cepheid star (bright)

△ The changing brightness of a Cepheid variable star, seen here on the left at its dimmest and on the right at its brightest, allows astronomers to measure the distance to the galaxies. After the discovery of this type of star, the painstaking mapping of the Universe, galaxy by galaxy, could begin.

△ The Local Group consists of about thirty galaxies. Our own spiral galaxy, the Milky Way, is surrounded by dwarf galaxies and a few irregular galaxies. To the right is the great Andromeda galaxy and its smaller companions, including the spiral M33. The other irregular galaxies are more isolated.

TYPE OF GALAXY

| *Dwarf galaxy* |
| *Irregular galaxy* |
| *Spiral galaxy* |

▽ *Fritz Zwicky discovered that galaxies are grouped in clusters, some of them thousands strong and millions of light years across.*

▽ *The* Hubble Space Telescope *revealed that the core of the Andromeda galaxy has a double nucleus. This may have resulted from a merger with another galaxy.*

◁ *The Andromeda galaxy has a spiral form similar to the Milky Way. Andromeda is 2.2 million light years away, and 150,000 light years across.*

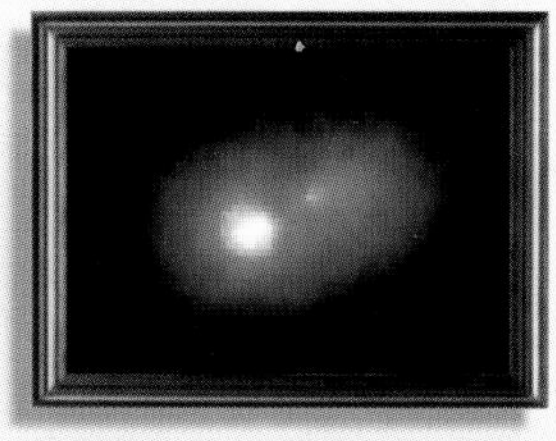

△ *Andromeda galaxy*

△ *Andromeda's core*

ANDROMEDA

M33

△ *Fritz Zwicky*

MILKY WAY

Rotating galaxies

The spiral shape of many galaxies gives the impression that they are rotating. However, it is not the stars that are going round and round, but the arms, with the stars passing through them. The arms rotate over hundreds of millions of years, their outside ends trailing behind the faster inner regions. In our own galaxy it takes the Sun over two hundred million years to complete an orbit and come back to the same position. This period is sometimes called the cosmic year.

Superclusters

Even the vast Local Group is a small backyard on the intergalactic scale. We are part of a much larger grouping of other clusters which together form the Local Supercluster. Our Local Group is being pulled by gravity towards the Virgo cluster, the centre of the Local Supercluster (sometimes also known as the Virgo Supercluster), at a speed of 270 kilometres per second. Superclusters are among the largest structures seen in the Universe, but even the Local Supercluster is just one of many others stretching billions of light years across the Universe.

Expanding Universe

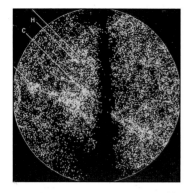

The speed of galaxies is one of the easier things to calculate in the Universe. The light from stars and galaxies comes with a very convenient measure. If a galaxy is moving away from us, the wavelength of its light is redshifted, or stretched. If it is coming towards us, the wavelength gets squashed and shifted towards the blue end of the spectrum. In 1929, Edwin Hubble discovered that the more distant a galaxy is, the more its light is redshifted. And it soon became clear that the further a galaxy is from our own, the faster it is speeding away. Hubble concluded that the reason for this is not that our galaxy is at the centre of the Universe, but rather that the entire Universe is expanding. If this is so, then there must have been a time when all the galaxies were much closer together.

△ *The dark, vertical band in this map of galaxies is where our own galaxy, the Milky Way, blocks the view. We are moving at 600 km/sec towards the Great Attractor, the dense, bright cluster near the centre.*

Mapping the Universe

By using redshift to measure the distances to galaxies, astronomers have begun to map the Universe in three dimensions. It is an enormous task but already some very large structures have been revealed. Some areas are like voids or bubbles with very few galaxies in them. Around them are slabs and filaments rich in galaxies. One particular structure forms what has been called the Great Wall, and is at least a billion light years across. There might be a repeating structure of such walls, a bit like a picket fence, with walls about 400 million light years apart.

▽ *On the largest scale, the Universe is like a vast foam, with superclusters and walls of galaxies situated along the boundaries of giant bubbles or voids in space.*

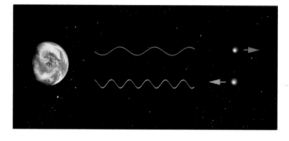

△ *If a galaxy or star is moving towards us, the waves in its light become squashed together, or blueshifted, and so it looks bluer. If, on the other hand, the object is receding from us, the light becomes stretched or redshifted.*

◁ *This slice through the Universe shows all the galaxies that have had their redshifts measured. Faint structures are visible. Black areas have not yet been fully surveyed.*

▽ *The 2DF instrument on the Anglo-Australian Telescope can measure the redshifts of up to 400 galaxies at once.*

The Great Attractor

The Universe does not expand evenly in every direction. Huge concentrations of galaxies put a gravitational brake on the process. Whole streams of galaxies end up resisting the expansion – we are part of such a stream. Beyond the great Virgo Supercluster there appears to be something pulling us and thousands of other galaxies towards it. It has been called the Great Attractor, and it lies in the approximate direction of the constellation Perseus. It acts as if it has a mass of fifty million billion suns, equivalent to hundreds of thousands of galaxies. At one time it was thought that the Great Attractor might be some monster black hole or other strange object. Now it is generally believed to be an irregularity, or a knot, in the clouds of galaxies. Even so, it has enough gravity to pull our whole local group of galaxies towards it at a velocity of about 600 kilometres per second.

△ *This image of the Andromeda galaxy has been colour coded to show the redshift and blueshift caused by the galaxy's rotation.*

The Galactic Zoo

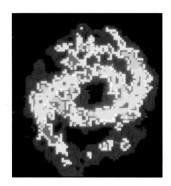

△ *Some galaxies, such as NGC 1300, appear to lose their tightly wound spiral structure as they evolve and develop a broad bar.*

The Universe contains around one hundred billion galaxies and each galaxy, on average, is made up of about one hundred billion stars. Galaxies come in many different shapes and sizes. Spiral galaxies can be tightly wound or loose, while others have a broad bar across their centre. Some galaxies have no obvious shape and are classed as irregular.

The largest of all galaxies are elliptical. Starbirth does not take place in elliptical galaxies. It could be that most galaxies begin as spirals but, as they interact with one another, all their gas is pulled into the stars. The spiral structure disappears and becomes an elliptical galaxy.

Looking back in time

The most distant galaxies ever seen are probably more than ten billion light years away. This means that light has taken ten billion years to reach us so what we are seeing is the light that left them when the Universe was ten billion years younger. By peering back across such distances, it is possible to see galaxies as they form. In one particular study by the *Hubble Space Telescope*, no less than 18 dwarf galaxies were spotted moving together under the influence of each other's gravity. This suggests that galaxies are formed when much smaller galaxies merge together. The final stages of this process can be seen today in our own galaxy as it swallows up a few remaining dwarf galaxies.

▷ *Astronomers believe that these faint smudges of starcluster, eleven billion light years away, are the building blocks that will merge to form the core of a new galaxy.*

◁ *Giant elliptical galaxies such as M49 are the final stage in galactic evolution. They contain almost no young stars.*

△ *The central hub of the whirlpool galaxy, M51, is made up mostly of old, yellow stars. The spiral arms contain young, blue stars while a bridge of gas and dust connects it to a second galaxy.*

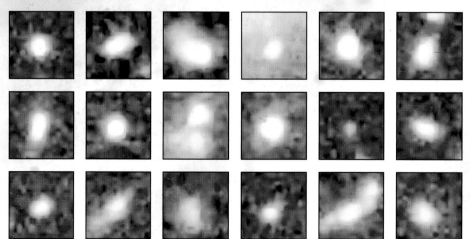

▽ M82 is a spiral galaxy, seen here almost edge-on. The disturbance at the centre is probably caused by the galaxy ploughing into a gas cloud.

Starburst

There must have been a time when the first stars started to shine, a spectacular period in the history of the Universe which had been dark since the Big Bang of creation. When astronomers peer through the great clouds of dust in which stars are made, they can see whole galaxies shining brightly with the sudden birth of millions of big, hot stars. More recent starburst galaxies are also seen where galaxies have smashed into one another, stirring up the dust lanes and triggering a new burst of star formation. In one of these, called Arp 220, the rate of star formation is probably a hundred times that of our entire Milky Way galaxy, but concentrated into a nucleus a hundred times smaller.

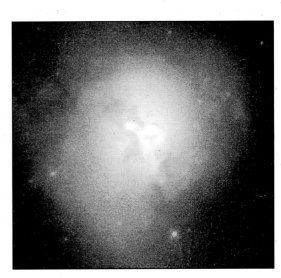

△ Arp 220 is a starburst galaxy, packed with very new, hot young stars. It probably formed when two spiral galaxies merged.

The Hubble Deep Field

In December 1995, the *Hubble Space Telescope* was pointed at a single stretch of sky for ten consecutive days. It revealed no less than 1,500 galaxies at various stages of evolution. Some are four billion times fainter than can be seen by the naked eye and date back to near the beginning of the Universe. This so-called Hubble Deep Field is beginning to give astronomers clues about how many galaxies there are in the Universe and how they formed.

△ This is what the Hubble Space Telescope *saw when it took a ten day exposure of a patch of sky close to the constellation of the Plough. The Hubble Deep Field is made up of 342 exposures and contains 1,500 galaxies, some of them among the faintest and most distant ever seen.*

Violent Galaxies

△ *The first quasar to be identified was 3C 273, viewed here in x-rays. Although star-like in appearance, quasars are very distant and intensely active galaxies.*

In 1963, Maartin Schmidt, an astronomer in California, was examining the spectrum of light from a faint, blue star-like object known as 3C 273. To his astonishment, he realized that, although it was small, it was more than three billion light years away, moving away from us at 50,000 kilometres per second and giving out intense radiation. These distant objects became known as quasi-stellar radio sources or quasars for short. The *Hubble Space Telescope* has revealed that quasars are, in fact, blindingly bright objects embedded in the centres of distant galaxies. They appear star-like because they emit a hundred times more energy than our entire galaxy, but from an area not much bigger than our Solar System.

Monster black holes

There is only one power source that could generate the immense energy of quasars – black holes. Most quasars are found in colliding galaxies. As the galaxies merge, gas and stars are stirred up and begin to spiral around a black hole that lies at the centre of one or even both galaxies. As matter is sucked in, an accretion disc is created, similar to those around black holes formed from dying stars in our own galaxy. But in the case of quasars, the black holes must be incredibly massive, each perhaps a billion times the mass of the Sun.

▽ *The galaxy M87, in the Virgo cluster, sends out a narrow jet of matter from its core. The activity in this galaxy is probably caused by a giant black hole.*

△ *A great cloud of swirling gas and star debris spirals down towards a black hole millions of times the mass of the Sun. At the same time it gives out x-rays and powerful jets of radio-emitting gas. Many of the violent processes taking place in the cores of galaxies are probably similar events seen from different angles.*

△ *In this computer simulation, two spiral galaxies have collided and passed one another. Spiral arms have been dragged out into a bridge of matter between them.*

Galactic activity

Not all galaxies fit into the neat classification of spiral, elliptical, irregular or even quasar. Many are being torn apart by immense explosions. Others, like M87 in the Virgo cluster, have a single great jet of matter spiralling out from the core. It seems likely that all these different galaxies have a massive black hole at their centre. In some cases the black hole becomes active each time it is fed with gas and stars. In other galaxies the black hole remains dormant. There is good reason to believe that every galaxy, including our own, has a black hole at its centre.

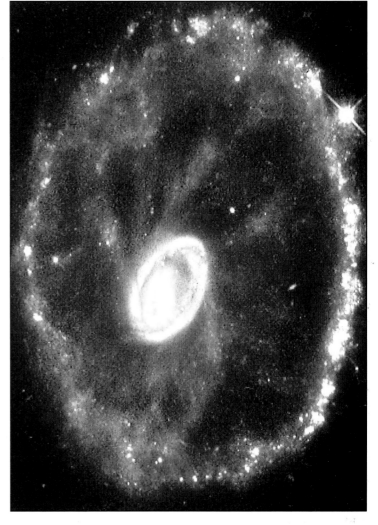

△ *The Cartwheel galaxy is the result of a collision in which one galaxy passed straight through the middle of another spiral galaxy.*

◁ *Light bent by gravity creates the illusion of a cluster of five different quasars when, in fact, there is only one. It is called Einstein's cross.*

Gravitational lens

When astronomers identified two identical quasars lying next to each other they were puzzled. The explanation quickly dawned – it was something first predicted by Einstein, who realized that light is bent by a strong gravitational field. If there is a massive object such as a cluster of galaxies between us and the quasar, the light from the quasar becomes bent, as if through a lens. If the alignment is right, light will be bent through several routes and create a multiple image. This can take the form, for example, of a cross or even a clover leaf.

Echoes of Creation

The Universe is flying apart. Trace all the lines of the expanding galaxies back in time and it appears they all originated from the same place. If so, they must have been blown apart by an incredible explosion. In the 1950s, the English astronomer Fred Hoyle and others suggested a different explanation. They argued that the Universe, though expanding, remains essentially the same, with new matter created to fill the expanding gaps. This is known as the 'Steady State' Universe and Fred Hoyle called the alternative the 'Big Bang' Universe. Other scientists remained unconvinced by Hoyle's theory and predicted that there should be a way of proving that the Big Bang had really happened. If the Universe did begin in an explosion, it would have left an echo. The incredible heat of the explosion would now have cooled to just a few degrees above absolute zero (−273°C), but even so it should be detectable.

COBE

−0.27

△ *The Cosmic Background Explorer satellite, COBE, was launched in 1990 to study the microwave background radiation left over from the Big Bang over twelve billion years ago. Scientists are now beginning to build up a quite detailed map of the early Universe.*

▽ *You can listen to the sound of the Big Bang in your own home! If you tune your television between stations, the picture will 'snow', and the sound will hiss. About one percent of this noise is from the microwave background reaching us from the Big Bang itself.*

Whispers from space

When the first transatlantic communications satellite, *Telstar*, was launched in 1962, a big radio antenna was constructed in New Jersey, United States, to receive its signal. But it also received a faint background hiss which would not go away even when two astronomers, Robert Wilson and Arno Penzias, removed pigeon droppings from the receiver! The hiss seemed to come from every direction and radiated energy at a temperature just 2.73 degrees above absolute zero. They realized that this must be the background radiation left from the Big Bang itself. To date, this is the best evidence that the Universe did indeed begin in a fireball.

$$r = T(e^{-uT} - 1)$$

▽ *The map of the cosmic background radiation is not a true map as some of the signal was due to warmth in COBE's instruments. Even so it confirmed that the present structure of the Universe originated in the Big Bang. When the discovery was made, the leader of the project described it as "like seeing the face of God".*

Cosmic ripples

In 1990, NASA launched *COBE*, the *Cosmic Background Explorer* satellite. Its purpose was to stare at the microwave background. The first result was a spectacular confirmation that the radiation is a perfect example of so-called 'black body' radiation — radiation that is simply due to heat. *COBE* then started to map it and look for features. The radiation turned out to be very, very smooth in every direction. Eventually, patterns began to emerge and, in 1992, scientists announced that they had seen ripples in the background. This caused a sensation. The fluctuations are only thirty millionths of a degree, but they provided the early Universe with enough variation in density for the very first stars and galaxies to be born. Without them, the Universe would still be a diffuse haze of gas.

DMR

+0.27

▽ *Robert Wilson and Arno Penzias stand in front of the radio antenna with which they discovered the microwave background radiation in 1962. The antenna was originally designed to pick up signals from the communications satellite, Telstar.*

First light

The fireball of the Big Bang gave off no light. Light could not travel in straight lines without bumping into things — atoms had not yet formed and the Universe was a seething mass of particles. After about 300,000 years, the Universe had cooled enough for atoms to form. The Universe became transparent and radiation could shine freely. The microwave background radiation is the cooled remnant of that first light.

△ *The discovery of the background radiation sent out ripples through astronomy. The theory of the Steady State Universe (which rejects the Big Bang theory) was finally discredited.*

The Big Bang

Astronomers can trace the expanding Universe back to a time when all the stars and galaxies they can see must have been squashed together into a tiny space. They can look back directly to the cosmic background radiation emitted when our Universe was about 300,000 years old and only slightly larger than our own galaxy. To journey back further, towards the Big Bang itself, it is necessary to turn to physics. Scientists have studied conditions back to within a hundredth of a billionth of a second of the start of the Universe by recreating them in high energy particle colliders. And their theories take them even further.

A note on scale

The numbers in cosmology are so vast and the numbers in sub-atomic physics are so tiny that scientists use a special shorthand. Ten multiplied by itself (ie a hundred) is written as 10^2. A thousand is 10^3. Similarly, a tenth is 10^{-1}, a thousandth 10^{-3} and so on.

△ *Einstein's famous equation E=mc² shows that it takes a lot of energy to make a little matter. In the first instant of the Big Bang (1) all four fundamental forces of Nature act as one, and even space and time are unified.*

△ *By 10^{-32} seconds (2), the Universe is a hot, seething mass of particles, expanding at the speed of light. At 10^{-11} seconds (3), the weak nuclear force separates from electromagnetism. Quarks and antiquarks are spontaneously created and annihilate each other.*

In the beginning

The entire Universe may have been born from a single sub-atomic particle! Today, every speck of seemingly empty space is a seething well of potential energy. Physicists suspect that a whole range of particles are being born from it every instant. Usually, they die again before they have had time to do anything, go anywhere or be seen by anyone. But, just occasionally, they can get trapped and become 'real'. No one really knows, but this is possibly how the Universe came into being.

Superforce

There are just four fundamental forces at work in the Universe – gravity, the strong and weak nuclear forces, and electromagnetism. But they may all have been united into a single superforce that governed the Universe at the moment of its birth. As the Universe cooled, so each of the forces separated. Gravity was the first to separate, at just 10^{-43} seconds after the start. The strong force followed at 10^{-35} seconds; the weak force and electromagnetism went their separate ways at 10^{-11} seconds.

▽ *After 300,000 years (6) radiation is no longer strong enough to break up atoms. The Universe becomes transparent and light shines through it. After one billion years (7) clumps of gas are pulling together to form protogalaxies. Inside them the first stars are beginning to shine.*

7

▽ *Today (8), after 12 billion years, clusters of galaxies have formed superclusters. Matter has been processed through several generations of stars to form the building materials for planets and life.*

8

△ *At 10^4 seconds (4), the Universe is about the size of the Solar System and the temperature has fallen sufficiently for quarks to form protons, neutrons and other so-called baryons. After 100 seconds (5), protons and neutrons link up.*

△ *The background image shows the tracks of subatomic particles. Scientists create these in high-energy collisions to explore conditions similar to those after the Big Bang.*

Inflation

A process called inflation might explain how something smaller than an atom grew to a universe the size of a grapefruit in the first 10^{-32} of a second. If a little bubble of the Universe continued expanding after the strong nuclear force should have separated out, it might have created a false vacuum, a sort of antigravity. This would allow the bubble to expand 100 times faster than the speed of light. When inflation froze, it released so much energy that it produced all the matter in our Universe.

First atom

When the strong force separated, the Universe heated up to 10^{27} degrees. Matter and antimatter were created in equal proportions. An imbalance in the process led to a build-up of matter, which is why there are no anti-galaxies today. The first particles were quarks and electrons. As the Universe cooled, quarks combined to form protons and neutrons. Some of them clustered together to make helium nuclei and, after 300,000 years, the electrons joined them to make the first atoms.

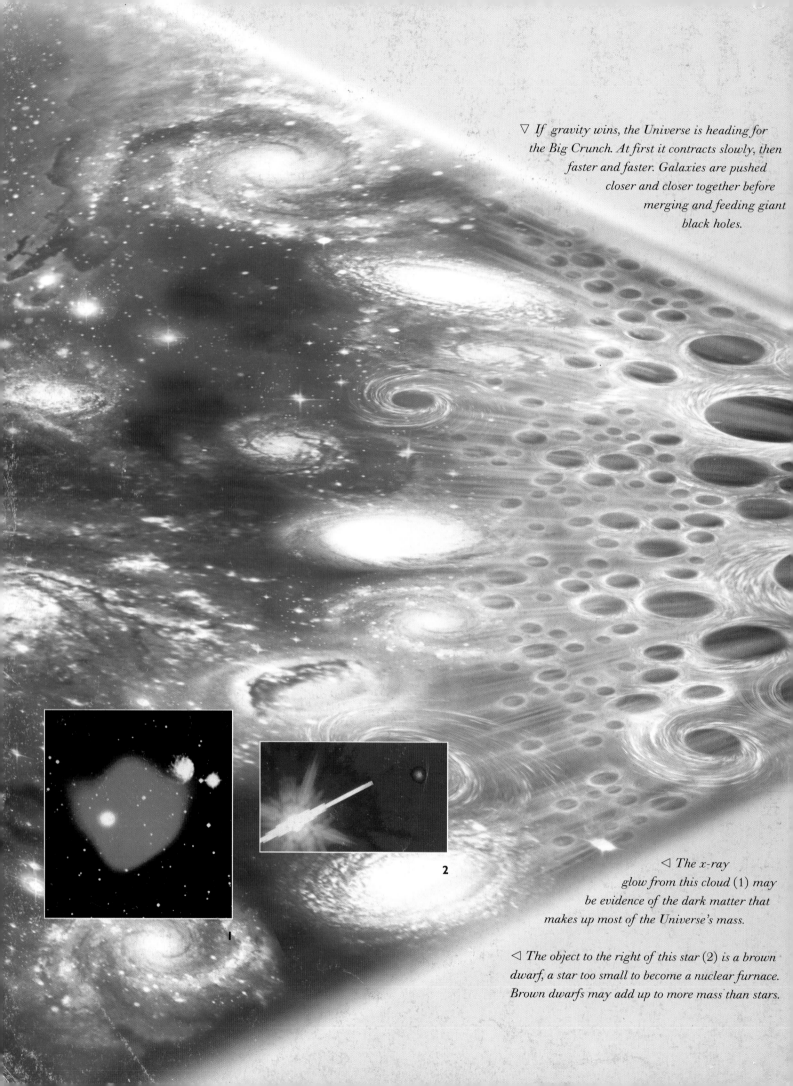

▽ *If gravity wins, the Universe is heading for the Big Crunch. At first it contracts slowly, then faster and faster. Galaxies are pushed closer and closer together before merging and feeding giant black holes.*

◁ *The x-ray glow from this cloud (1) may be evidence of the dark matter that makes up most of the Universe's mass.*

◁ *The object to the right of this star (2) is a brown dwarf, a star too small to become a nuclear furnace. Brown dwarfs may add up to more mass than stars.*

The Great Unknown

There are some questions about the nature of the Universe that, until recently, seemed to be unanswerable. What makes up the Universe? How heavy is it? How old is it, and how will it all end? Astronomers still do not have all the answers, but at last they feel they might be able to begin to find out. To do so will take some very strange telescopes indeed. As well as using the best measurements possible from optical, infrared and radio telescopes on the ground and in space, there are also instruments deep underground attempting to weigh the Universe and predict its ultimate fate.

△ *The Universe could end in three ways. The closed or Big Crunch Universe (1) is so massive it collapses under its own weight. In the flat Universe (2) expansion slows down, but never quite into collapse. The open Universe (3) expands forever.*

◁ *As the Universe approaches its end, the remaining matter spirals into black holes. Nothing can hold the Universe back from the final inferno. But perhaps it could bounce back in a new Big Bang.*

Dark matter

All that we can see is only a fraction of the Universe. Some matter is detectable only by its gravitational effects on the rotation of galaxies. This is called dark matter and no one knows its composition. Dark matter could be conventional matter, such as small stars called brown dwarfs, or even black holes.

Ghostly particles

Dark matter may also include neutrinos – ghostly particles once thought to have no mass. These are so numerous that any mass at all would make them far heavier than all the stars. Other particles are predicted by physicists, but are yet to be detected. If found they could make up ninety-nine percent of the Universe.

The fate of the Universe

From its birth, now thought to be between twelve and fifteen billion years ago, the Universe has continued to expand. It would take a hundred times more mass than is contained in the visible Universe to halt this expansion altogether. If this happened, the Universe would contract into the Big Crunch. This could be the end of everything or the start of a new Universe.

Heat death

Other evidence suggests that the Universe is not sufficiently dense to halt the expansion. Stars will slowly age and die. Galaxies will fade away and even black holes will disappear. After billions and billions of years the Universe will become a cold, dull place, containing only a few, widely-spaced particles.

△ Alice enters a wormhole in space-time. It could take her to another time, or even into another universe.

△ Space itself can be curved, so a wormhole might act as a short-cut between two seemingly distant places.

△ Time appears to run in one direction only. Broken eggs do not reassemble themselves. This tendency to disorder is one of the few natural arrows in time.

Beyond Time

Time is relative. The rate your clock ticks relative to someone else's depends on how fast you are moving relative to each other. This was the conclusion Albert Einstein came to in 1905. He established that, as the speed of light must be the same for everyone, no matter how they are moving, then space and time themselves must be intertwined. Einstein developed these ideas in his general theory of relativity, taking gravity into account and showing how gravity bends space-time. Many science-fiction writers and some scientists have seized on Einstein's theories to show that one day time travel may just be possible.

Time's arrow

We all have a strong sense of passing time, and for all of us time seems to run in one direction only. People age, cups of tea cool down, smashed glasses do not spontaneously reassemble. However, according to the laws of physics, there is nothing to prevent most processes from reversing. In fact, in many processes, especially at the level of particles, there is no distinguishable arrow of time.

Warping space and time

The fundamental speed limit of the Universe seems to be the speed of light – 300,000 km per second. Even though a spaceship could never travel faster than light it might, in theory, be possible to warp the space around it, shrinking space ahead and expanding it behind. The snag is that to distort space in this way would require at least a million times the energy locked up in the Sun!

▷ *Tweedledum and Tweedledee are identical twins. Tweedledum sets out on a round trip to a nearby star, at almost the speed of light. The journey seems to him to have taken only a few years. When he returns he finds that time has passed more quickly for Tweedledee, who is now twenty years older.*

Wormholes

One possibility for time travel, in theory at least, is a wormhole – a cosmic tunnel built from exotic matter between different regions of space-time. Just as in a black hole, time in a wormhole slows to a standstill and the laws of our Universe break down. But if one could be kept open long enough, it might be possible to emerge from a wormhole unharmed.

Time paradoxes

Time travel raises many paradoxes. For example, if you could travel back in time, you would have the chance to kill your own grandfather before your father was born. That would mean that you also were never born, so how could you begin your journey? Either reverse time travel is forbidden or there are an infinite number of universes, one for every possibility. Perhaps it is simpler to stick to the here and now!

▷ *When Alice steps through the wormhole, she appears instantaneously in another part of the Universe.*

The Search for ET

Are people on the Earth alone in the Universe? As yet, there is no certain evidence of life anywhere else, much less intelligent life. But there are hundreds of millions of stars in our galaxy. If a fraction have habitable planets and a fraction of those developed life, there could be millions of civilizations other than our own. However, the distances between the stars is so great it is unlikely that extra-terrestrials – if they exist – have visited our planet. We do not even know exactly how life began on the Earth. The evidence we do have, however, suggests that it takes several billion years of evolution for intelligent life to arise and to develop the technology capable of sending messages to the stars.

△ *The plaque fixed to* Voyager 1 *describes where it comes from and who built it. It also carries a record of natural sounds of the Earth as well as music.*

The search for distant planets

Our best telescopes could never see a distant planet against the glare of its star. But big planets make stars wobble as they orbit and several wobbling stars have been detected. Most are due to big, Jupiter-like planets, but some may be far enough away from their stars to be hospitable. Far out in space, away from the dust in the inner Solar System, arrays of telescopes may in the future see planets directly as they orbit other stars. They may even be able to detect gases, such as ozone and water vapour, that indicate life.

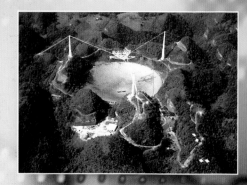

△ *In 1974, the first signal to possible alien life was broadcast from the world's biggest radio dish at Arecibo in Puerto Rico. Arecibo has remained the centre for the search to identify alien signals.*

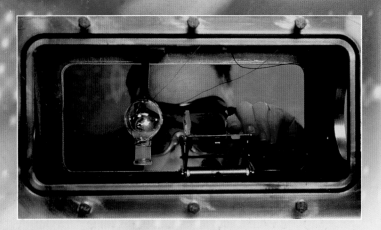

△ *A scientist discharges an electric field across a mixture of water, hydrogen, methane and ammonia. In this experiment, amino acids – the basis of life on this planet – accumulate after a time, just as they may once have done on the early Earth.*

The search for extra-terrestrial intelligence

Since the first radio broadcast, radio signals have been travelling out beyond our planet at the speed of light. The signals have passed many stars and planets, but unless aliens were listening for them they would not notice. The most powerful radio signal to have left the Earth was sent from a radio telescope at Aricebo, Puerto Rico, in 1974. It was a brief digital signal describing who and where we are, and it was directed at a cluster of stars known as M13. Even at the speed of light, however, it will take 25,000 years to reach its destination. Many teams are taking part in SETI (the Search for Extra-Terrestrial Intelligence). They scan Sun-like star systems with radio telescopes, analyzing millions of radio frequencies by computer in the search for a signal.

Will aliens look like these mounds
bacteria? Similar structures may have
n among the first inhabitants of the
rth more that 3,500 million years ago.

△ Alien existence is a subject
clouded by fiction and fraud.
The 'flying saucer' above was
proved to be a child's toy
photographed at close range.
Though many people claim to
have been visited or abducted
by aliens, there is still no
evidence of the presence of
other beings in the Universe.

Alien life on other planets

If there are aliens out there, what would they be like?
Life on the Earth shows great variety and ingenuity and it
is probable that life on another planet would do the same.
It might be based on a different chemistry entirely, with
boron or silicon taking the place of carbon, or with the role
of water being played by liquid ammonia. Physically, life
forms will need to do some of the same things as humans.
They may need to move about, sense their environment,
eat and defend themselves. They would probably have a
front and a back, but eyes, hands and so on could all be
replaced by other tools, and not necessarily in pairs.

△ This bright light was photographed over
São Paulo, Brazil in 1984. It is one of many
so-called UFOs – Unidentified Flying Objects.

Impossible Questions

Throughout this book we have seen how astronomers observe our planet, our solar system, our galaxy and some of the billions of other galaxies beyond it. One day, in principle, we could learn every detail of the physical Universe. But there are still some questions that can never be answered with certainty. For example, what lies beyond or before our Universe? Why did the Universe begin? Why are we here in it? Astronomy, in discovering that the Earth is not the centre of the Universe, has pushed us further and further into what seems an insignificant corner. But some of the possible answers to these big questions could put us centre stage again.

△ *Every culture has proposed a god as the prime mover of the Universe. Scientists can offer few better explanations for the fundamental laws of the cosmos.*

Beyond the horizon

The furthest galaxies seem to be receding from us so fast that they are approaching the speed of light. We cannot see beyond them. The Universe may be infinite, or it may end just beyond this light horizon. We cannot tell. Perhaps our Universe is just one bubble in a whole foam of universes. Some may not have inflated, while others might have different physical laws or dimensions from our own Universe.

The living Universe

Perhaps, when a black hole forms in our Universe, it gives birth to another universe somewhere else. If the new universe can inherit the ability to make black holes, then universes might evolve and get better and better at making black holes. A universe, like our own, which is good at creating black holes is also good at making stars and ultimately planets and life itself.

▷ *Black holes may give birth to new universes. The coloured peaks in this computer simulation are other universes, each with its own physical laws.*

▽ The same force that makes apples fall also holds stars together. The same force that makes things radioactive blows the elements out from exploding stars to form new stars and planets. The same force that gives us electricity also makes the Universe transparent, enabling us to study it. It is as if we were meant to be.

Cosmic coincidences

Life may seem a lottery, the Universe a random accident. Perhaps the biggest coincidence of all is that our Universe is just right for life. If, for example, beryllium nuclei, made in the cores of stars, were a different size, they would not go on to form carbon and oxygen, elements essential for life. If the weak nuclear force was slightly different, stars would not explode as supernovae, spewing their elements out to form potential new stars and planets. But if the force of gravity was slightly stronger all stars would collapse into black holes. The list goes on, raising the question of whether our Universe is meant to be the way it is.

The ultimate question

The final question is why we are here? Cosmologists point out how the Universe is finely tuned to complexity and life. This is called the weak anthropic principle. More controversially it has also been suggested that this is more than coincidence and that the Universe *must* produce intelligent observers. Some even argue that observers are necessary to bring the Universe into being and that ultimately everything there is must be known. If that is true, astronomy has a bright future and we are back at the centre of the Universe.

▽ On a small, blue planet, the third rock from an average star in a typical spiral galaxy, a life form developed with the potential to understand the Universe. Why?

Universal Facts

THE PLANETS OF THE SOLAR SYSTEM

NAME	DISTANCE FROM SUN (Million km)	DIAMETER (km)	MASS (Earth=1)	ROTATION	YEAR	MOONS
Mercury	57.91	4,878	0.055	58.66 days	87.97 days	0
Venus	108.2	12,103	0.81	243.01 days	224.7 days	0
Earth	149.6	12,756	1.00	23.93 hrs	365.26 days	1
Mars	227.9	6,786	0.11	24.62 hrs	686.98 days	2
Jupiter	778.3	142,984	318	9.92 hrs	11.86 years	16
Saturn	1427	120,536	95.18	10.67 hrs	29.46 years	23
Uranus	2871	51,118	14.50	17.23 hrs	84.01 years	15
Neptune	4497	49,528	17.14	16.12 hrs	164.79 years	8
Pluto	5914	2,284	0.0022	6.375 days	248.54 years	1

BRIGHTEST STARS (in order of apparent brightness)

NAME	TYPE	LOCATION	DISTANCE (Light years)	APPARENT MAGNITUDE	ABSOLUTE MAGNITUDE
Sirius	White Major	Canis	8.6	-1.46	1.4
Canopus	Yellow Giant	Carina	1200	-0.72	-8.5
Alpha Centauri	Yellow	Centaurus	4.3	-0.27	4
Arcturus	Orange Giant	Botes	36	-0.04	-0.2
Vega	White	Lyra	25	0.03	0.5
Capella	Yellow	Auriga	43	0.08	-0.7
Rigel	Blue Giant	Orion	900	0.12	-7.1
Procyon	Yellow Minor	Canis	11	0.38	2.6
Achernar	Blue Giant	Erudanus	85	0.46	-1.6
Betelgeux	Red Giant	Orion	310	0.5	5.6
Agena	Blue Giant	Centaurus	460	0.61	-5.1
Altair	White	Aquila	17	0.77	2.2
Acrux	Binary	Southern Cross	360	0.83	-3.9
Aldebaran	Orange	Taurus	68	0.85	-0.3
Antares	Red Giant	Scorpius	330	0.96	-4.7
Spica	Blue Giant	Virgo	260	0.98	-3.6
Pollux	Orange Giant	Gemini	36	1.14	0.2
Fomalhaut	White	Piscis Australis	22	1.16	2.0
Deneb	White Giant	Cygnus	1800	1.25	-7.5
Beta Crucis	Blue Giant	Southern Cross	425	1.25	-5.0
Regulus	Blue	Leo	85	1.35	-0.6

FIRSTS IN ASTRONOMY

1600BC	Babylonian star catalogues compiled
270BC	Aristarchos proposes the Earth revolves around the Sun
230BC	Eratosthenes measures the Earth's circumference
135BC	Hipparchos discovers that the Earth's axis wobbles
AD127	Ptolemy develops the Earth-centred theory of the Universe
1054	Chinese observe the Crab supernova
1543	Copernicus revives the idea of a Sun-centred Universe
1609	Kepler describes the orbits of planets
1609	Galileo is first to use a telescope for astronomy
1655	Huygens discovers Saturn's rings
1668	Newton makes first reflecting telescope
1687	Newton publishes Theory of Gravitation
1705	Halley recognizes that comets orbit the Sun
1781	Herschel discovers Uranus
1838	Bessel measures the distance of a star
1846	Adams and Leverrier predict existence of Neptune
1912	Leavitt discovers Cepheid variable stars
1920	Slipher discovers that nebulae are receding
1923	Hubble shows that receding nebulae are galaxies
1938	Bethe and Weizsäcker suggest stars are powered by nuclear fusion
1963	Schmidt discovers the first quasar
1965	Penzias and Wilson discover microwave background radiation
1967	Jocelyn Bell discovers first pulsar
1992	COBE satellite identifies ripples in the microwave background

Note: The lower the value of the magnitude, the brighter the star.

Apparent magnitude is how bright the star seems from the Earth.

Absolute magnitude is how bright it would seem if all the stars were the same distance from the Earth.

MAJOR TELESCOPES - optical/infrared

NAME	LOCATION	DIAMETER	FIRST LIGHT
VLT	Chile	16 m equivalent	1998
Keck	Hawaii, USA	2 x 10 m	1990
Mt Hopkins	Arizona, USA	6.5 m	1998
Zelenchukskaya	Russia	6 m	1976
Hale, Palomar	California, USA	5 m	1948
Herschel	Canary Islands	4.2 m	1987
Cerro Tololo	Chile	4.0 m	1976
Mayall	Arizona, USA	3.8 m	1973
Anglo-Australian	Australia	3.9 m	1975
UK InfraRed	Hawaii, USA	3.8 m	1978
Hubble	Space	2.4 m	1990

MAJOR PLANETARY PROBES

NAME	NATION	LAUNCH	TARGET	RESULT
Mariner 2	USA	1962	Venus	First fly-by
Venera 3	USSR	1965	Venus	Crushed during descent
Mariner 4, 6 & 7	USA	1964, '69, '69	Mars	Fly-bys
Venera 7	USSR	1970	Venus	Landed. Survived 23 mins
Mars 2 & 3	USSR	1971	Mars	2: Orbiter, dropped flag 3: Orbiter and Lander
Mariner 9	USA	1971	Mars	Orbiter
Pioneer 10	USA	1972	Jupiter	Fly-by 1973
Pioneer 11	USA	1973	Jupiter and Saturn	Jupiter fly-by 1974 Saturn fly-by 1979
Viking 1 & 2	USA	1975	Mars	Orbiters and Landers
Voyager 1	USA	1977	Jupiter and Saturn	Jupiter fly-by 1979 Saturn fly-by 1980
Voyager 2	USA	1977	Grand Tour	Fly-bys: Jupiter 1979, Saturn 1981, Uranus 1986, Neptune 1989
Pioneer Venus	USA	1978	Venus	Orbiter
Venera 13	USSR	1981	Venus	Landed, lasted 2 hours
Venera 15	USSR	1983	Venus	Radar mapper
Vega 1	USSR	1984	Venus	Lander and balloon, plus Halley's comet fly-by
Magellan	USA	1989	Venus	Radar mapper
Galileo	USA	1989	Jupiter	Orbiter plus probe. Arrived 1995
Pathfinder	USA	1996	Mars	Lander & rover
Global Surveyor	USA	1996	Mars	Mapping orbiter
Cassini	USA/Europe	1997	Saturn	Orbiter & Titan probe

FIRSTS IN SPACE

1957   Sputnik 1 (USSR) first satellite launched

1958   Explorer 1 (USA) discovers Van Allen radiation belts

1959   Luna 1 (USSR) escapes Earth's gravity

1959   Vanguard 2 (USA) takes first photos of the Earth

1959   Luna 2 (USSR) hits the Moon

1959   Luna 3 (USSR) returns first pictures of far side of the Moon

1960   TIROS 1 (USA) first weather satellite

1960   ECHO 1 (USA) first communications satellite

1961   Vostok 1 (USSR) first manned orbital flight

1962   Aerobee (USA) x-ray satellite launched

1963   Vostok 6 (USSR) carries first woman in orbit

1965   Early Bird (USA) commercial geostationary communications satellite

1965   Gemini 6 (USA) manned rendezvous in space

1966   Luna 9 (USSR) soft Moon landing

1969   Apollo 11 (USA) manned lunar landing

1975   Apollo/Soyuz first international link-up

1978   Launch of International Ultraviolet Explorer (USA/EUROPE)

1981   Columbia (USA) first Space Shuttle flight

1986   Launch of Mir space station

1990   Hubble Space Telescope (USA/EUROPE) launched

1998   Launch of first component of International Space Station

Glossary

Accretion disc A disc of matter that builds up around a dense object as material spirals down towards it. It is believed that accretion discs often form around black holes.

Antimatter A form of matter that shares properties with the fundamental particles of matter but in reverse, such as an opposite electrical charge.

Asteroid A rocky or metallic minor planet orbiting the Sun. Most asteroids lie between the orbits of Mars and Jupiter in the asteroid belt.

Astronomical Unit The average distance between the Earth and the Sun (149,597,870 km). It is a useful unit for expressing distances in the Solar System.

Atmosphere A layer of gas surrounding a planet, star or a moon.

Billion One thousand million (1,000,000,000).

Binary star A pair of stars in orbit around the common centre of gravity between them (i.e. around each other).

Black hole A region of space-time where there is such a concentration of matter, and consequently gravity, that not even light can escape. Black holes can form when massive stars collapse. Others lie at the heart of active galaxies.

Brown dwarf A small star of such low mass (less than 8 percent of the Sun's mass) that nuclear fusion reactions cannot begin. A brown dwarf shines only because of the faint heat released as it contracts.

Cepheid variable A class of star that varies its brightness in a regular period between one and fifty days.

Cluster A group of stars or galaxies affecting each other by their gravitational attraction.

Comet An object made of ice, dust and other material. There may be billions of comets beyond the orbit of Pluto. Some come nearer the Sun, on elliptical orbits, leaving spectacular tails of gas and dust.

Constellation A grouping of stars in the same direction in the sky, though not necessarily associated with each other.

Corona The outer atmosphere of the Sun, extending many millions of kilometres above the visible surface. The corona can reach 2,000,000°C and is visible during eclipses.

Cosmic background radiation Microwave radiation coming from all directions in the sky and thought to be the cooled remnant of the fireball of the Big Bang in which the Universe began.

Cosmology The study of the structure and origin of the Universe.

Crater Circular depression on a planet, moon or asteroid, usually resulting from the impact of another body.

Dark matter Matter known to exist, but mostly invisible. It might be normal matter in the form of brown dwarfs or black holes, or it could be ghostly, unidentified particles.

Eclipse A shadow cast by one celestial object on another. For example, the Earth's shadow falling on the Moon causes a lunar eclipse. The Moon's shadow falling on the Earth is seen as a solar eclipse.

Escape velocity The velocity that a projectile must reach if it is to escape from the gravity of an astronomical object without further propulsion.

Event horizon The boundary around a black hole from within which neither matter nor radiation can escape.

False-colour Colour added by computer to enhance the details of an image.

Galaxy A celestial city of millions or billions of stars, gas and dust bound together by their gravitational pull.

Gamma rays The most energetic radiation in the electromagnetic spectrum.

Globular cluster A spherical cluster of between a few thousand and a million stars. Globular clusters form the halo of our galaxy and contain very ancient stars.

Gravitational lens A region of mass, such as a cluster of galaxies, which bends light from more distant objects.

Gravity An attractive force between matter dependent on mass. Although weak, gravity acts over large distances.

Hubble constant The rate at which the Universe is expanding. As the galaxies move further apart, this causes redshift which can be used to measure the rate of expansion.

Infrared radiation Electromagnetic radiation with a longer wavelength than red light but less than radio.

Light year The distance that light travels in one year. (9,460,700,000,000 km).

Local Group The grouping of about 30 galaxies in which our own galaxy is found.

Magnetosphere The magnetic bubble around the Earth or another planet in which ionized gas is controlled by the planet's magnetic field.

Main sequence The range of temperature and brightness at which the majority of stars spend most of their lives.

Meteor A brilliant streak across the sky caused by objects, such as specks of dust or rocks, burning up as they enter the Earth's atmosphere. Meteors are popularly known as shooting stars.

Meteorite A lump of rock or metal that has fallen to the Earth from space. The largest meteorites create craters on impact.

Nebula A cloud of gas or dust in space.

Neutrino A particle with no charge and little or no mass.

Neutron star A star that has been so compressed that electrons and protons have been squashed together to make neutrons. It has the mass of a star but the size of a city.

Oort Cloud A cloud of millions or even billions of dormant comets thought to lie beyond the orbit of Pluto.

Orbit The path of one body around another, such as the Moon around the Earth or the Earth around the Sun. It may be circular, or more often, elliptical.

Parallax The apparent motion of an object against a more distant background caused by a changing viewpoint. It provides a basis for calculating the distances to nearby stars.

Perihelion The closest point to the Sun in the orbit of a body such as a comet or planet.

Photon The smallest particle of energy that can be carried as light.

Planet A body in orbit around the Sun or another star, shining in reflected light only. Bodies over 1,000 km across are normally considered to be planets. Smaller objects are called minor planets.

Planetary Nebula A cloud of gas that can look like a planet but really consists of expanding shells of gas thrown off by a star close to the end of its life.

Protostar An early stage in the formation of a star before nuclear fusion has begun.

Pulsar A spinning neutron star emitting bursts of radiation, like a flashing lighthouse beam, often many times a second.

Quasar The energetic core of an active galaxy. Quasars give out as much energy as a big galaxy from a region no bigger than our solar system. Quasar is short for quasi-stellar object.

Red dwarf A small, dim red star with a temperature of less than 5,000°C.

Red giant A bright red star up to 100 times the diameter of the Sun and thought to be near the end of its life.

Redshift The stretching of light from an object, such as a galaxy, that is moving away from us. Because the Universe is still expanding, the higher the redshift, the more distant the object.

Satellite Any object in orbit around another object. The term is normally applied to a moon or an artificial craft orbiting around a planet.

Solar wind The stream of electrically-charged particles blowing from the Sun. When it strikes molecules of air in the Earth's atmosphere, it produces the curtain of light known as the aurora.

Space-time The combination of the three dimensions of space plus one of time. Space-time makes up the fabric of the Universe.

Spectrum The rainbow band of electromagnetic radiation of different wavelengths. The light from a star or galaxy, split up into its wavelengths of different colours.

Sub-atomic physics The study of the fundamental particles that make up atoms, and the forces that act between them.

Sunspot A dark spot on the surface, or photosphere, of the Sun, caused by a magnetic disturbance. A sunspot is slightly cooler than the surrounding area.

Supercluster A grouping made up of clusters of galaxies. Superclusters can be hundreds of millions of light years across.

Supernova An exploding, massive star torn apart by an intense flash of radiation. This happens when the core of a star collapses.

Ultraviolet radiation Electromagnetic radiation of shorter wavelength than the blue end of the visible spectrum.

Universe Space-time and everything contained within it. In theory, there might be universes other than our own, but we could no have no direct knowledge of them, or they would be part of our own universe.

Van Allen belts The belts of radiation around the Earth caused by charged particles trapped in the Earth's magnetic field.

Wavelength The distance between successive peaks (or troughs) in a wave, such as electromagnetic radiation.

White dwarf A hot, compact star no heavier than 1.4 times the mass of the Sun. With most of its nuclear fuel used up, the star contracts until it is very dense and hot.

X-rays Electromagnetic radiation of shorter wavelength than ultraviolet radiation.

Index

Acknowledgements

The publishers would like to thank the following illustrators for their contribution to this book:

Julian Baum 6–7, 10–11 (*background*), 24–25, 26–27, 29*cr* & *br*, 30*tl* & *bl*, 31*tr*, 32–33, 34–35, 36*tl*, 37*br*, 38–39, 40–41, 42–43, 44–45, 46–47, 48–49, 50–51, 52–53, 54–55, 56*tl*, 57*tr*, 58–59, 60–61, 65*br*, 66*bl*, 68–69, 72–73, 76–77; **Jim Burns** 12–13, 14–15; **Tom Connell** 13*br*, 14*tl*, 15*br*, 16*b*, 17*tl*; **Bernard Gudynas/ZAP ART** Icons, 20–21, 66–67, 70–71, 84–85, 88–89;

Peter Gudynas/ZAP ART 22–23, 78–79, 80–81, 82–83, 86–87; **Ceri Llewellyn** 9*bl*, 37*cl*, 56*br*, 59*cl*, 62*tl*.

The publishers would also like to thank the following: Clarissa Claudel, Peter Clayman, Sarah Goodwin, Ian Graham, Justin Hobson at the Science Photo Library, Charlotte Hurdman, Pauline Newman, Robin Redfern, Camilla Reid, Miranda Smith, Julie Tatnell, Marc Wilson.

The publishers would like to thank the following for supplying photographs:

Page 6 Zefa *tl*, Science Photo Library *tr*, Bridgeman Art Library *c*; 7 Science Photo Library *t*, Corbis UK *c*; 8 Scala *tl*, Carnegie Institute of Washington *bl*, Mary Evans Picture Library *cr*; Getty Images *background image*; 9 Science Photo Library *tl*, Galaxy Picture Library *tr*, Frank Spooner Pictures *br*; 10 Planet Earth Pictures *tr*, NASA *cr*, ESA *bl*; 11 NASA *tr*, ESA *cr*, ESA *bc*; 12 Planet Earth Pictures *l*, E.T. Archive *tc*, Popperfoto *tr*, Corbis UK *c*; 13 Novosti *tl*, Science Photo Library *tc*, Frank Spooner Pictures *cr*; 14 NASA *bl*, Frank Spooner Pictures *bc*; 13 Genesis Space Picture Library *c*; 16 Frank Spooner Pictures *tl*, Telegraph Colour Library *bl*; 16/17 Frank Spooner Pictures; 17 Science Photo Library *bl*, ESA *c*, Science Photo Library *br*; 18 Science Photo Library *tl*, Science Photo Library *bc*, NASA *b*, Novosti *cr*; 18/19 NASA *c*; 19 NASA/Portfolio Pictures *tr*, Science Photo Library *cl*, Galaxy Picture Library *cr*, Science Photo Library *bl*; 20 Galaxy Picture Library *bl*, Popperfoto *bc*, Telstar *tr*, ESA/Meteosat *tc*; 21 NASA/Mir/Hubble/ERS *t*, ESA/Exosat *bl*, Landsat 4/Planet Earth Pictures *c*, Getty Images *br*; 22 Meteosat/ESA *tl*, Planet Earth Pictures *tc*, Science Photo Library *cr*, Science Photo Library *bl*, 23 NASA *tc*, Science Photo Library *bc*, Frank Spooner Pictures *br*; 26 Science Photo Library *tl*, Galaxy Picture Library *cl*; 27 Science Photo Library *t*; 28/29 Science Photo Library; 30 Science Photo Library *cl*; 30/31 Science Photo Library *c*;

Bruce Coleman *b*; 31 ESA *bc*, Robert Harding Associates *br*; 32 Science Photo Library *tl*, Planet Earth Pictures *tr*, Planet Earth Pictures *bc*; 32/33 Science Photo Library *c*; 33 NASA *background image*; 34 Science Photo Library *tl*, *bl*; 35 Science Photo Library *cl*, Planet Earth Pictures *cr*, Galaxy Picture Library *tc*, Science Photo Library *c*, NASA *tr*, Science Photo Library *cr*, Planet Earth Pictures *br*, Planet Earth Pictures *background image*; 36 Science Photo Library *bl*; 37 Planet Earth Pictures *tl*, Ronald Grant *background image*, Science Photo Library *tr*, Galaxy Picture Library *c*; 38 Science Photo Library; 39 Zefa/Stockmarket *tc*; National Air Photo Library of Canada *tr*, Natural History Museum, London *bl*, Galaxy Picture Library *cl*, Natural History Museum, London *b*; 40 Science Photo Library *cl*, NASA/Jet Propulsion Laboratory/USA, Science Photo Library *br*; 41 NASA/Jet Propulsion Laboratory *tl*, Planet Earth Pictures *tr*, NASA/Jet Propulsion Laboratory *cr*, Galaxy Picture Library *b*; 42 Planet Earth Pictures *bl*; Planet Earth Pictures *tr*; 41 Planet Earth Pictures *tl*, Galaxy Picture Library *cr*, *br*; 44 Planet Earth Pictures *tl*, Galaxy Picture Library *bl*, Science Photo Library *cr*, *bl*; 45 Science Photo Library *tl*, NASA/Jet Propulsion Laboratory *br*; 48 Science Photo Library bl, Galaxy Picture Library *br*; 49 Galaxy Picture Library *tc*, *tr*, *cr*, Telegraph Colour Library *bl*; 50/51 Galaxy Picture Library; 52 Science Photo Library *tl*, Galaxy Picture Library *cl*; 53 Galaxy Picture Library *tl*, Planet Earth Pictures *bl*; 54 Ann Ronan @ Image Select *tl*, Science Photo Library *cl*,

Galaxy Picture Library *bl*, Science Photo Library *br*; 55 E.T. Archive *tl*, Science Photo Library *bl*; 56/57 Science Photo Library; 58 Telegraph Colour Library *bl*, Science Photo Library br; 59 Martin Redfern *tl*, Science Photo Library *tr*; 60 Galaxy Picture Library *bl*, Martin Redfern/NASA/S. Stolovy, University of Arizona *br*; 61 Martin Redfern/HST/NASA Jeff Hester & Paul Scowen, Arizona State University *cl*; Martin Redfern/NASA/C.R. O'Dell; 62 Galaxy Picture Library *bl*, Science Photo Library *cr*; 63 Science Photo Library *cl*, Martin Redfern *br*; 64 Science Photo Library *tl*, Science Photo Library *bl*, Royal Observatory, Edinburgh *background image*, NASA/Peter Garnavich, Harvard-Smithsonian Center for Astrophysics *cr*; 64/65 Martin Redfern; 65 Science Photo Library *bl*, Science Photo Library *tr*; 66/67 original illustrations by John Tenniel from *Alice's Adventures In Wonderland* by Lewis Carroll; 68 Science Photo Library; 69 Planet Earth Pictures *tr*, Science Photo Library *cl*, *cr*, Martin Redfern *br*; 70 Science Photo Library; 71 Galaxy Picture Library *t*, Neils Bohr Library/USA *b*; 78 Science Photo Library *tr*; 78/79 Planet Earth Pictures; 79 Science Photo Library *b*; 80/81 Science Photo Library *background image*; 82 Science Photo Library *bl*, 84 original illustrations by John Tenniel from *Through the Looking Glass* by Lewis Carroll; 86 NASA/Jet Propulsion Laboratory *tl*, Science Photo Library *bl*, Planet Earth Pictures *cr*; 86/87 Science Photo Library; 87 Fortean Picture Library *br*; 88 *The Ancient of Days* by William Blake *tl*; 89 Pictor International *bl*; **Endpapers** Getty Images.